H. P. BLAVATSKY
to the
American Conventions
1888-1891

H. P. BLAVATSKY
to the
American Conventions
1888-1891

with a
Historical Perspective
BY KIRBY VAN MATER

Theosophical University Press
PASADENA, CALIFORNIA

THEOSOPHICAL UNIVERSITY PRESS
PASADENA, CALIFORNIA 91109
1979

Copyright © 1979 by Theosophical University Press

All rights including the right of reproduction in whole or in part in any form are reserved under International and Pan American Copyright Conventions.

Library of Congress Catalog Card Number 78-74256

ISBN 0-911500-88-x

Manufactured in the United States of America

Contents

Foreword — vii

H. P. BLAVATSKY TO THE AMERICAN CONVENTIONS

   I Chicago, 1888 — 1

  II Chicago, 1889 — 13

 III Chicago, 1890 — 23

 IV Boston, 1891 — 31

  V Boston, 1891 — 41

HISTORICAL PERSPECTIVE — 47
  by *Kirby Van Mater*

INDEX — 71

Foreword

"Do as the gods when incarnated do. Feel yourselves the vehicles of the whole humanity, mankind as part of yourselves, and act accordingly" — stirring words which are the keystone of a series of letters addressed by H. P. Blavatsky to the American theosophists during the last four years of her life. Scarcely known outside the theosophical world, these letters are classics in their own right; first, because of their historic value, in that they were sent during a period of intense activity when the Theosophical Society, from a mere handful in 1875, had spread from America to Europe and Asia; and secondly, though not less significant, because of their extraordinary relevance to the present cycle: as we read her words, we feel as though they had been written with this century in mind, so cogently do they respond to the need for sound guidance in the wake of today's spiritual and psychic upheaval.

H. P. Blavatsky has been called the Sphinx of the 19th century, and today is still an enigma. That she was a great deal more than she appeared to be, even to her close associates, is self-evident. This is reason enough to study her writings with the eye of intuition. The progress of her life and work had by no means been smooth; while remarkable advances were being made, grave crises both for H.P.B. and for the Society had to be met, from without as well as from within. But theosophy had sent down roots deep into the soil of human consciousness, and no slander or betrayal had power to destroy that which was destined to live.

This was a movement of the spirit, impulsed in the closing decades of the 19th century by H. P. Blavatsky's teachers, Friends of humanity, whose principal concern had been to establish a viable outlet in the modern world that would have the stamina to carry over into the succeeding centuries. For this they needed an instrument, an amanuensis willing and able to transmit the wisdom-teachings of the ages in a fuller and more comprehensive form than had been possible for thousands of years. Moreover, they had to find and train someone whose love for the disinherited of soul as well as of body and mind was all-consuming.

These letters show H. P. Blavatsky in her true light — as the voice of her teachers, the bearer of a message of supreme spiritual worth: that divinity is intrinsic to every life-spark throughout the cosmos and not an isolated phenomenon possible only to a Christ; that man and the whole of nature are *one*, in essence, origin, and goal; that in consequence all entities have the same potential for growth and unfoldment, through cyclic change and renewal of form; and, of chief import, that brotherhood is universal, and its *living* practice by all nations and races a necessity if present civilization is to fulfill its promise.

At the writing of the first letter, little more than a dozen years had gone by since 1875, yet already theosophic ideas were being picked up by writers and thinkers and effecting a marked change in the spirit of the times. Nonetheless, theosophy in its simple purity had still an "uphill battle," and the American members were reminded that the Theosophical Society, whose first principle is universal brotherhood, was founded to stimulate the spiritual awakening of mankind, and not "as a nursery for forcing a supply of Occultists." H. P. Blavatsky and her teachers had foreseen the growing force of transcendentalism, following upon the wave of mere phenomenalism, that would sweep over the coming decades and quicken a spiritual and intellectual revival. They had also recognized the hazards attendant upon its advance if the psychism now fast developing in America was allowed to run rampant and not held under the control of man's nobler faculties. It is ethics, she declared, the grand moral truths of theosophy, that are "even more necessary to mankind than the scientific aspects of the psychic facts of nature and man," since their practice penetrates to the inner reaches of the soul, to endure in the eternal essence, whereas the cultivation of the psychic alone is of transient worth.

How prophetic her words are in light of the proliferation of astral and psychic gadgetry sought today by an eager public, all of which tends to cast a shadow of mistrust on "the real students of the psychic sciences," among whom today may be found a number of well-moti-

FOREWORD

vated and creative researchers into the inner levels of man's consciousness. Again and again H. P. Blavatsky exhorts her American colleagues to seize the opportunities that are theirs, and to work together to help guide the rising tide of psychic sensitivity, expected at this period of our racial growth, so that "it may finally work for good and not for evil."

To read these letters, one after the other — the last two written just three and a half weeks before she died — is to sense something of the urgency felt by the Mahatmas in the 1870s to get these ennobling truths into circulation once again among every class of minds. They knew that time was needed for the ideals of compassion and of the *oneness* of all living beings to permeate the consciousness of the 20th century *before* the tidal wave of psychic interest and development would overwhelm humanity. We intuit also why it was that after searching for nearly a century they selected H. P. Blavatsky to be their agent for the founding of a movement whose sacred obligation would be "to change the basis of men's lives from selfishness to altruism."

In their initial choice they included as first president Henry S. Olcott. Without his executive talent and profound humanitarian spirit to create a vehicle for the dynamic genius of Helena Petrovna Blavatsky, the theosophical effort might not have had the success it did — to become within her lifetime a thriving organization able to extend its influence to every quarter of the globe. He remained to the end of his life steadfast in devotion to the "common cause — that of helping mankind."

When it came, however, to establishing the Esoteric Section in 1888, in response to a call from the membership and as a means of strengthening the inner core of the Theosophical Society, H. P. Blavatsky turned to her American brother and co-founder, William Q. Judge. To relate intelligently this move and others to the flow of events of the closing years of her life, and also to give background to the letters themselves, Kirby Van Mater, archivist for the Theosophical Society (Pasadena), has provided a Historical Perspective. In presenting certain of the salient elements in the Society's experience in its formative stages, he has exercised great care in the assemblage of documents so as to allow the facts themselves to reveal the powerful current of inspiration that impulsed the theosophic effort through H. P. B.

It was no small accomplishment to have launched into a dogma-ridden world the very truths for which others had died in past eras. Yet this is what H. P. Blavatsky achieved. Since her day, generations of theosophists have drawn courage from the heroism and sacrifice of Helena Blavatsky, and have voluntarily taken upon themselves to share in the responsibility of the ages: to change for the better the mental and spiritual climate of world consciousness. Through their fidelity and perceptiveness the effort initiated by the Adepts in 1875 lives on, and the life-giving truths they gave forth anew are today being sought by a growing number of seekers in quest of a philosophy that both inspires and consistently challenges.

June 15, 1979
Pasadena, California

GRACE F. KNOCHE

1888

Second Annual Convention — April 22–23
American Section of the Theosophical Society
Sherman House, Chicago, Illinois

Letter from H. P. Blavatsky, dated April 3,
read by William Q. Judge, afternoon session, April 22

Reproduced verbatim from the original typescript in the
Archives of the Theosophical Society, Pasadena

My dearest Brother and Co-Founder of the Theosophical Society;

In addressing to you this letter, which I request you to read to the Convention summoned for April 22d, I must first present my hearty congratulations and most cordial good wishes to the assembled Delegates and good Fellows of our Society, and to yourself - the heart and Soul of that Body in America. We were several, to call it to life in 1875. Since then you have remained alone to preserve that life through good and evil report. It is to you chiefly, if not entirely, that the Theosophical Society owes its existence in 1888. Let me then thank you, for the first, and perhaps for the last, time, publicly, and from the bottom of my heart, which beats only for the cause you represent so well and serve so faithfully. I ask you also to remember that, on this important occasion, my voice is but the feeble echo of other more sacred voices, and the transmitter of the approval of Those whose presence is alive in more than one true Theosophical heart, and lives, as I know, preeminently in yours. May the assembled Society feel the warm greeting as earnest-ly as it is given, and may every Fellow present, who realises that he has deserved it, profit by the Blessings sent.

To WILLIAM Q. JUDGE,
   General Secretary of the American Section of the Theosophical Society.

MY DEAREST BROTHER AND CO-FOUNDER OF THE THEOSOPHICAL SOCIETY;

In addressing to you this letter, which I request you to read to the Convention summoned for April 22d, I must first present my hearty congratulations and most cordial good wishes to the assembled Delegates and good Fellows of our Society, and to yourself — the heart and soul of that Body in America. We were several, to call it to life in 1875. Since then you have remained alone to preserve that life through good and evil report. It is to you chiefly, if not entirely, that the Theosophical Society owes its existence in 1888. Let me then thank you for it, for the first, and perhaps for the last, time publicly, and from the bottom of my heart, which beats only for the cause you represent so well and serve so faithfully. I ask you also to remember that, on this important occasion, my voice is but the feeble echo of other more sacred voices, and the transmitter of the approval of Those whose presence is alive in more than one true Theosophical heart, and lives, as I know, preeminently in yours. May the assembled Society feel the warm greeting as earnestly as it is given, and may every Fellow present, who realizes that he has deserved it, profit by the Blessings sent.

Theosophy has lately taken a new start in America which marks the commencement of a new Cycle in the affairs of the Society in the West. And the policy you are now following is admirably adapted to give scope for the widest expansion of the movement, and to establish on a firm basis an organization which, while promoting feelings of fraternal sympathy, social unity, and solidarity, will leave ample room for individual freedom and exertion in the common cause — that of helping mankind.

The multiplication of local centers should be a foremost consideration in your minds, and each man should strive to be a center of work in himself. When his inner development has reached a certain point, he will naturally draw those with whom he is in contact under the same influence; a nucleus will be formed, round which other people will gather, forming a center from which information and spiritual influence radiate, and towards which higher influences are directed.

But let no man set up a popery instead of Theosophy, as this would be suicidal and has ever ended most fatally. We are all fellow students, more or less advanced; but no one belonging to the Theosophical Society ought to count himself as more than, at best, a pupil-teacher — one who has no right to dogmatize.

Since the Society was founded, a distinct change has come over the spirit of the age. Those who gave us commission to found the Society foresaw this, now rapidly growing, wave of transcendental influence following that other wave of mere phenomenalism. Even the journals of Spiritualism are gradually eliminating the phenomena and wonders, to replace them with philosophy. The Theosophical Society led the van of this movement; but, although Theosophical ideas have entered into every development or form which awakening spirituality has assumed, yet Theosophy pure and simple has still a severe battle to fight for recognition. The days of old are gone to return no more, and many are the Theosophists who, taught by bitter experience, have pledged themselves to make of the Society a "miracle club"* no longer. The fainthearted have asked in all ages for signs and wonders, and

---

[*In May 1875, Colonel Olcott attempted to organize "a private investigating committee under the title of the 'Miracle Club,'" to study psychic phenomena. The project failed. In her "Scrap Book" (vol. 1, p. 27), H. P. Blavatsky wrote that this attempt was made on orders received at this time "to begin telling the public the *truth* about the phenomena & their mediums." See *Old Diary Leaves*, vol. 1, p. 25; also *H. P. Blavatsky: Collected Writings*, vol. 1, pp. 88-9. — K.V. M.]

when these failed to be granted, they refused to believe. Such are not those who will ever comprehend Theosophy pure and simple. But there are others among us who realize intuitionally that the recognition of pure Theosophy — the philosophy of the rational explanation of things and not the tenets — is of the most vital importance in the Society, inasmuch as it alone can furnish the beacon-light needed to guide humanity on its true path.

This should never be forgotten, nor should the following fact be overlooked. On the day when Theosophy will have accomplished its most holy and most important mission — namely, to unite firmly a body of men of all nations in brotherly love and bent on a pure altruistic work, not on a labor with selfish motives — on that day only will Theosophy become higher than any nominal brotherhood of man. This will be a wonder and a miracle truly, for the realization of which Humanity is vainly waiting for the last 18 centuries, and which every association has hitherto failed to accomplish.

Orthodoxy in Theosophy is a thing neither possible nor desirable. It is diversity of opinion, within certain limits, that keeps the Theosophical Society a living and a healthy body, its many other ugly features notwithstanding. Were it not, also, for the existence of a large amount of uncertainty in the minds of students of Theosophy, such healthy divergencies would be impossible, and the Society would degenerate into a sect, in which a narrow and stereotyped creed would take the place of the living and breathing spirit of Truth and an ever growing Knowledge.

According as people are prepared to receive it, so will new Theosophical teaching be given. But no more will be given than the world, on its present level of spirituality, can profit by. It depends on the spread of Theosophy — the assimilation of what has been already given — how much more will be revealed, and how soon.

It must be remembered that the Society was not founded as a nursery for forcing a supply of Occultists — as a factory for the manufactory of Adepts. It was intended to stem the current of materialism, and also that of spiritualistic phenomenalism and the worship of the Dead. It had to guide the spiritual awakening that has now begun, and not to pander to psychic cravings which are but another form of materialism. For by "materialism" is meant not only an anti-philosophical negation of pure spirit, and, even more, materialism in conduct and action — brutality, hypocrisy, and, above all, selfishness — but also the fruits of a disbelief in all but material things, a disbelief which has increased enormously during the last century, and which has led many, after a denial of all existence other than that in matter, into a blind belief in the *materialization of Spirit*.

The tendency of modern civilization is a reaction towards animalism, towards a development of those qualities which conduce to the success in life of man as an animal in the struggle for animal existence. Theosophy seeks to develop the human nature in man in addition to the animal, and at the sacrifice of the superfluous animality which modern life and materialistic teachings have developed to a degree which is abnormal for the human being at this stage of his progress.

Men cannot all be Occultists, but they can all be Theosophists. Many who have never heard of the Society are Theosophists without knowing it themselves; for the essence of Theosophy is the perfect harmonizing of the divine with the human in man, the adjustment of his god-like qualities and aspirations, and their sway over the terrestrial or animal passions in him. Kindness, absence of every ill feeling or selfishness, charity, goodwill to all beings, and perfect justice to others as to oneself, are its chief features. He who teaches Theosophy preaches the gospel of goodwill; and the converse of this is true also — he who preaches the gospel of goodwill, teaches Theosophy.

This aspect of Theosophy has never failed to receive due and full recognition in the pages of the "PATH," a journal of which the American Section has good reason to be proud. It is a teacher and a power; and the fact that such a periodical should be produced and supported in the United States speaks in eloquent praise both of its Editor and its readers.

America is also to be congratulated on the increase in the number of the Branches or Lodges which is now taking place. It is a sign that in things spiritual as well as things temporal the great American Republic is well fitted for independence and self-organization. The Founders of the Society wish every Section, as soon as it becomes strong enough to govern itself, to be as independent as is compatible with its allegiance to the Society as a whole and to the Great Ideal Brotherhood, the lowest formal grade of which is represented by the Theosophical Society.

Here in England Theosophy is waking into new life. The slanders and absurd inventions of the Society for Psychical Research have almost paralyzed it, though only for a very short time, and the example of America has stirred the English Theosophists into renewed activity. "Lucifer" sounded the reveille, and the first fruit has been the founding of the "Theosophical Publication Society." This Society is of great importance. It has undertaken the very necessary work of breaking down the barrier of prejudice and ignorance which has formed so great an impediment to the spread of Theosophy. It will act as a recruiting agency for the Society by the wide distribution of elementary literature on the subject, among those who are in any way prepared to give ear to it. The correspondence already received shows that it is creating an interest in the subject, and proves that in every large town in England there exist quite enough isolated Theosophists to form groups or Lodges under charter from the Society. But, at present, these students do not even know of each other's existence, and many of them have never heard of the Theosophical Society until now. I am thoroughly satisfied of the great utility of this new Society, composed as it is to a large extent of members of the Theosophical Society, and being under the control of prominent Theosophists, such as you, my dear Brother W. Q. Judge, Mabel Collins, and the Countess Wachtmeister.

I am confident that, when the real nature of Theosophy is understood, the prejudice against it, now so unfortunately prevalent, will die out. Theosophists are of necessity the friends of all movements in the world, whether intellectual or simply practical, for the amelioration of the condition of mankind. We are the friends of all those who fight against drunkenness, against cruelty to animals, against injustice to women, against corruption in society or in government, although we do not meddle in politics. We are the friends of those who exercise practical charity, who seek to lift a little of the tremendous weight of misery that is crushing down the poor. But, in our quality of Theosophists, we cannot engage in any one of these great works in particular.

As individuals we may do so, but as Theosophists we have a larger, more important, and much more difficult work to do. People say that Theosophists should show what is in them, that "the tree is known by its fruit." Let them build dwellings for the poor, it is said, let them open "soup kitchens," etc., etc., and the world will believe that there is something in Theosophy. These good people forget that Theosophists, as such, are poor, and that the Founders themselves are poorer than any, and that one of them, at any rate, the humble writer of these lines, has no property of her own, and has to work hard for her daily bread whenever she finds time from her Theosophical duties. The function of Theosophists is to open men's hearts and understandings to charity, justice, and generosity, attributes which belong specifically to the human kingdom and are natural to man when he has developed the qualities of a human being. Theosophy teaches the animal-man to be a human-man; and when people have learnt to think and feel as truly human beings should feel and think, they will act humanely, and works of charity, justice, and generosity will be done spontaneously by all.

Now with regard to the "SECRET DOCTRINE," the publication of which some of you urged so kindly upon me, and in such cordial terms, a while ago. I am very grateful for the hearty support promised and for the manner in which it was expressed. The MSS. of the first three volumes is now ready for the press; and its publication is only delayed by the difficulty which is experienced in finding the necessary funds. Though I have not written it with an eye to money, yet, having left Adyar, I must live and pay my way in the world so long as I remain in it. Moreover, the Theosophical Society urgently needs money for many purposes, and I feel that I should not be justified in dealing with the "SECRET DOCTRINE" as I dealt with "ISIS UNVEILED." From my former work I have received personally in all only a few hundred dollars, although nine editions have been issued. Under these circumstances I am endeavoring to find means of securing the publication of the "SECRET DOCTRINE" on better terms this time, and here I am offered next to nothing. So, my dearest Brothers and Co-workers in the trans-Atlantic lands, you must forgive me the delay, & not blame me for it but the unfortunate conditions I am surrounded with.

I should like to revisit America, and shall perhaps do so one day, should my health permit. I have received pressing invitations to take up my abode in your great country which I love so much for its noble freedom. Colonel Olcott, too, urges upon me very strongly to return to India, where he is fighting almost single-handed the great and hard fight in the cause of Truth; but I feel that, for the present, my duty lies in England and with the Western Theosophists, where for the moment the hardest fight against prejudice and ignorance has to be fought. But whether I be in England or in India, a large part of my heart and much of my hope for Theosophy lie with you in the United States, where the Theosophical Society was founded, and of which country I myself am proud of being a citizen. But you must remember that, although there must be local Branches of the Theosophical Society, there can be no local Theosophists; and just as you all belong to the Society, *so do I belong to you all*.

I shall leave my dear Friend and Colleague, Colonel Olcott, to tell you all about the condition of affairs in India, where everything looks favorable, as I am informed, for I have no doubt that he also will have sent his good wishes and congratulations to your Convention.

Meanwhile, my faraway and dear Brother, accept the warmest and sincerest wishes for the welfare of your Societies and of yourself personally; and while conveying to all your Colleagues the expression of my fraternal regards, assure them that, at the moment when you will be reading to them the present lines, I shall — if alive — be in Spirit, Soul and Thought amidst you all.

>Yours ever, in the truth of the GREAT CAUSE
>we are all working for —
>
>H. P. BLAVATSKY

London. April 3. 1888.
17 Lansdowne Road.

I shall leave my dear Friend and Colleague, Colonel Olcott, to tell you all about the condition of affairs in India, where everything looks favourable, as I am informed, for I have no doubt that he also will have sent his good wishes and congratulations to your Convention.

Meanwhile, my faraway and dear Brother, accept the warmest and sincerest wishes for the welfare of your Societies and of yourself personally; and while conveying to all your Colleagues the expression of my fraternal regards, assure them that, at the moment when you will be reading to them the present lines, I shall – if alive – be in Spirit, Soul and Thought amidst you all.

Yours ever, in the truth of the Great Cause we are all working for —

H. P. Blavatsky

London. April 9. 1888.
17 Lansdowne Road.

II

1889

Third Annual Convention — April 28–29
American Section of the Theosophical Society
Palmer House, Chicago, Illinois

Letter from H. P. Blavatsky, dated April 7, read
by William Q. Judge, morning session, April 28

Reproduced verbatim from the printed
Report of Proceedings, pp. 14–20

17 LANSDOWNE ROAD, HOLLAND PARK, LONDON, W.
April 7, 1889

Friends and Brother Theosophists:

You are now once again assembled in Convention, and to you again I send my heartiest greetings and wishes that the present Convention may prove a still greater success than the last.

It is now the fourteenth year since the Theosophical Society was founded by us in New York, and with steady persistence and indomitable strength the Society has continued to grow amid adverse circumstances, amid good report and evil report. And now we have entered on the last year of our second septenary period, and it is fitting and right that we should all review the position which we have assumed.

In India, under Col. Olcott's care, Branches continue to be formed, and wherever the President lectures or pays a visit, a new center of interest is sure to be created. His visits in the spirit which animates him are like a shower of rain to thirsty, sun-parched soil; flowers and herbs spring up in profusion, and the seed of healthy vegetation is sown. Now he is on a visit to Japan, whither he was invited by a strong and influential deputation to lecture on Theosophy and Buddhism, among a people who are mad and crazy to acquire Western civilization; who believe that it can only be obtained by the suicidal adoption of Christianity as a national religion. Aye! to neglect their own natural national religion in favor of a parasitic growth — and for Western civilization with its blessings such as they are!

Truly young Japan is like the conceited Greek before Troy:

"We boast ourselves to be much better men than our fathers."

I have heard with regret that though Col. Olcott meditated a visit and a lecturing tour in America after his visit to Japan, his visit has unavoidably been prevented.

Here in England we have been hard at work; we have met some difficulties and surmounted them, but others, like the Hydra-heads of the labors of Hercules, seem to spring up at every step that is made. But a firm will and a steadfast devotion to our great Cause of Theosophy must and shall break down every obstacle until the stream of Truth shall burst its confines and sweep every difficulty away in its rolling flood. May Karma hasten the day.

But you in America. Your Karma as a nation has brought Theosophy home to you. The life of the Soul, the psychic side of nature, is open to many of you. The life of altruism is not so much a high ideal as a matter of practice. Naturally, then, Theosophy finds a home in many hearts and minds, and strikes a resounding harmony as soon as it reaches the ears of those who are ready to listen. There, then, is part of your work: to lift high the torch of the liberty of the Soul of Truth that all may see it and benefit by its light.

Therefore it is that the Ethics of Theosophy are even more necessary to mankind than the scientific aspects of the psychic facts of nature and man.

With such favorable conditions as are present in America for Theosophy, it is only natural that its Society should increase rapidly and that Branch after Branch should arise. But while the organization for the spread of Theosophy waxes large, we must remember the necessity for consolidation. The Society must grow proportionately and not *too* rapidly, for fear lest, like some children, it should overgrow its strength and there should come a period of difficulty and danger when natural growth is arrested to prevent the sacrifice of the organism. This is a very real fact in the growth of human beings, and we must carefully watch lest the "Greater Child" — the Theosophical Society — should suffer for the same cause. Once before was growth checked in connection with the psychic phenomena, and there may yet come a time when the moral and ethical foundations of the Society may be wrecked in a similar way. What can be done to prevent such a thing is for each Fellow of the Society to make Theosophy a vital factor in their lives

— to make it real, to weld its principles firmly into their lives — in short, to make it their own and treat the Theosophical Society as if it were themselves. Following closely on this is the necessity for Solidarity among the Fellows of the Society; the acquisition of such a feeling of identity with each and all of our Brothers that an attack upon one is an attack upon all. Then consolidated and welded in such a spirit of Brotherhood and Love we shall, unlike Archimedes, need neither fulcrum nor lever, but we shall move the world.

We need all our strength to meet the difficulties and dangers which surround us. We have external enemies to fight in the shape of materialism, prejudice, and obstinacy; the enemies in the shape of custom and religious forms; enemies too numerous to mention, but nearly as thick as the sand-clouds which are raised by the blasting Sirocco of the desert. Do we not need our strength against these foes? Yet, again, there are more insidious foes, who "take our name in vain," and who make Theosophy a byword in the mouths of men and the Theosophical Society a mark at which to throw mud. They slander Theosophists and Theosophy, and convert the moral Ethics into a cloak to conceal their own selfish objects. And as if this were not sufficient, there are the worst foes of all — those of a man's own household — Theosophists who are unfaithful both to the Society and to themselves. Thus indeed we are in the midst of foes. Before and around us is the "Valley of Death," and we have to charge upon our enemies — right upon his guns — if we would win the day. Cavalry — men and horses — can be trained to ride almost as one man in an attack upon the terrestrial plane; shall not we fight and win the battle of the Soul, struggling in the spirit of the Higher Self to win our divine heritage?

Let us, for a moment, glance backwards at the ground we have passed over. We have had, as said before, to hold our own against the Spiritists, in the name of Truth and Spiritual Science. Not against the students of the true psychic knowledge, nor against the enlightened Spiritualists; but against the lower order of phenomenalists — the blind worshipers of illusionary phantoms of the Dead. These we have fought for the sake of Truth, and also for that of the world which they were misleading. I repeat it again: no "fight" was ever waged against the real students of the psychic sciences. Professor Coues did much last year to make plain our real position, in his address to the Western Society for Psychic Research. He put in plain language the real importance of psychic studies, and he did excellent work in also laying stress upon the difficulties, the dangers, and, above all, the responsibilities of their pursuit. Not only is there a similarity, as he showed, between such pursuits and the manufacture of dangerous explosives — especially in unskilled hands — but the experiments, as the Professor truly said, are conducted on, with, and by a human soul. Unless prepared carefully by a long and special course of study, the experimentalist risks not only the medium's soul but his own. The experiments made in Hypnotism and Mesmerism at the present time are experiments of unconscious, when not of conscious, Black Magic. The road is wide and broad which leads to such destruction; and it is but too easy to find; and only too many go ignorantly along it to their own destruction. But the practical cure for it lies in one thing. That is the course of study which I mentioned before. It sounds very simple, but is eminently difficult; for that cure is "*ALTRUISM.*" And this is the keynote of Theosophy and the cure for all ills; this it is which the real Founders of the Theosophical Society promote as its first object — *UNIVERSAL BROTHERHOOD.*

Thus even if only in name a body of Altruists, the Theosophical Society has to fight all who under its cover seek to obtain magical powers to use for their own selfish ends and to the hurt of others. Many are those who joined our Society for no other purpose than curiosity. Psychological phenomena were what they sought, and they were unwilling to yield one iota of their own pleasures and habits to obtain them. These very quickly went away empty-handed. The Theosophical Society has never been and never will be a school of promiscuous Theurgic rites. But there are dozens of small occult Societies which talk very glibly of Magic, Occultism, Rosicrucians, Adepts, etc. These profess much, even to giving the key to the Universe, but end by leading men to a blank wall instead of the "Door of the Mysteries." These are some of our most insidious foes. Under cover of the philosophy of the Wisdom-Religion they manage to get up a mystical jargon which for the time is effective and enables them, by the aid of a very small amount of clairvoyance, to fleece the mystically inclined but ignorant aspirants to the occult, and lead them like sheep in almost any direction. Witness the now notorious H. B. of L., and the now famous G. N. K. R.* But woe to those who try to convert a noble philosophy into a den for disgusting immorality, greediness for selfish power, and money-making under the cloak of Theosophy. Karma reaches them when least expected. But is it possible for our Society to stand by and remain respected, unless its members are prepared, at least in future, to stand like one man, and deal with such slanders upon themselves as Theosophists, and such vile caricatures of their highest ideals, as these two pretenders have made them?

But in order that we may be able to effect this working on behalf of our common cause, we have to sink all private differences. Many are the energetic members of the Theosophical Society who wish to work and work hard. But the price of their assistance is that all the work must be done in their way and not in any one else's way. And if this is not carried out they sink back into apathy or leave the Society entirely, loudly declaring that they are the only true Theosophists. Or, if they remain, they endeavor to exalt their own method of working at the expense of all other earnest workers. This is fact, but it is not Theosophy. There can be no other end to it than that the growth of the Society will soon be split up into various sects, as many as there are leaders, and as hopelessly fatuous as the 350 odd Christian sects which exist in England alone at the present time. Is this prospect one to look forward to for the Theosophical Society? Is this "Separateness" consonant with the united Altruism of Universal Brotherhood? Is this the teaching of our Noble MASTERS? Brothers and Sisters in America, it is in your hands to decide whether it shall be realized or not. You work and work hard. But to work properly in our Great Cause it is necessary to forget all personal differences of opinion as to how the work is to be carried on. Let each of us work in his own way

---

[*"H.B. of L." stands for "Hermetic Brotherhood of Luxor," a spurious "esoteric" society which had its beginnings about 1884 in England, and later spread to America. "G.N.K.R.," whose initials represent "Genii of Nations, Knowledge(s), and Religion(s)," was another such bogus organization which was exposed as fraudulent in the Boston and New York press in February 1889. See "The Astral Plague and Looking-Glass" by G. R. S. Mead, *Lucifer*, September 1889, pp. 54–64; also *The Path*, August 1889, pp. 150–52. — K. V. M.]

and not endeavor to force our ideas of work upon our neighbors. Remember how the Initiate Paul warned his correspondents against the attitude of sectarianism they took up in the early Christian Church: — "I am of Paul, I of Apollos," and let us profit by the warning. Theosophy is essentially unsectarian, and work for it forms the entrance to the Inner life. But none can enter there save the man himself in the highest and truest spirit of Brotherhood, and any other attempt at entrance will either be futile or he will lie blasted at the threshold.

But Karma will reconcile all our differences of opinion. A strict account of our actual work will be taken, and the "wages" earned will be recorded to our credit. But as strict an account will be taken of the work which any one, by indulging in personal grievances, may have hindered his neighbors from doing. Think you it is a light thing to hinder the force of the Theosophical Society, as represented in the person of any of its leaders, from doing its appointed work? So surely as there is a Karmic power behind the Society will that power exact the account for its hindrance, and he is a rash and ignorant man who opposes his puny self to it in the execution of its appointed task.

Thus, then, "UNION IS STRENGTH"; and for every reason private differences must be sunk in united work for our Great Cause.

Now what has been our work during the past year? Here we have organized the British Section of the Theosophical Society with the help and under the orders of the President-Founder, Col. Olcott. And instead of one Lodge have been formed smaller local Branches, which, therefore, have greater powers of work and facilities of meeting. What has been done in India you will probably have already heard. And you have heard or know what has been accomplished and what increase in strength your own Section has made.

As regards our means of spreading knowledge, we have in the West "Lucifer," the "Path" and the T. P. S. pamphlets. All these have brought us into contact with numerous persons of whose existence we should not otherwise have become aware. Thus they are all of them necessary to the Cause, as is also the attempting to influence the public mind by the aid of the general Press. I regret to say that several co-workers on "Lucifer" have now left it and the Society for precisely such personal differences as those alluded to above, and have now become antagonistic, not only to me personally, but to the system of thought which the Theosophical Society inculcates.

On account of a personal feeling against Col. Olcott, the "Lotus" — the French Journal — has also seceded from Theosophy; but we have just founded "La Revue Théosophique" to replace it in Paris. It is edited by myself and managed or directed by Countess d'Adhémar, an American lady, loved and respected by all who know her, and a friend of our Brother, Dr. Buck.

As many of you are aware, we have formed the "Esoteric Section." Its members are pledged, among other things, to work for Theosophy under my direction. By it, for one thing, we have endeavored to secure some solidarity in our common work: to form a strong body of resistance against attempts to injure us on the part of the outside world, against prejudice against the Theosophical Society and against me personally. By its means much may be done to nullify the damage to the work of the Society in the past and to vastly further its work in the future.

Its name, however, I would willingly change. The Boston scandals have entirely discredited the name "Esoteric"; but this is a matter for after consideration.

Thus, as I have already said, our chief enemies are public prejudice and crass obstinacy from a materialistic world; the strong "personality" of some of our own members; the falsification of our aims and name by money-loving charlatans; and, above all, the desertion of previously devoted friends who have now become our bitterest enemies.

Truly were those words wise which are attributed to Jesus in the Gospels. We sow our seed and some falls by the wayside on heedless ears; some on stony ground, where it springs up in a fit of emotional enthusiasm, and presently, having no root, it dies and "withers away." In other cases the "thorns" and passions of a material world choke back the growth of a goodly fruitage, and it dies when opposed to the "cares of life and the deceitfulness of riches." For, alas, it is only in a few that the Seed of Theosophy finds good ground and brings forth a hundredfold.

But our union is, and ever will be, our strength, if we preserve our ideal of Universal Brotherhood. It is the old "In hoc signo vinces"

["With this sign thou shalt conquer"] which should be our watchword, for it is under its sacred flag that we shall conquer.

And now a last and parting word. My words may and will pass and be forgotten, but certain sentences from letters written by the Masters will never pass, because they are the embodiment of the highest practical Theosophy. I must translate them for you: —

" * * * Let not the fruit of good Karma be your motive; for your Karma, good or bad, being one and the common property of all mankind, nothing good or bad can happen to you that is not shared by many others. Hence your motive, being selfish, can only generate a double effect, good and bad, and will either nullify your good action, or turn it to another man's profit." * * "There is no happiness for one who is ever thinking of Self and forgetting all other Selves."

"The Universe groans under the weight of such action (Karma), and none other than self-sacrificial Karma relieves it. * How many of you have helped humanity to carry its smallest burden, that you should all regard yourselves as Theosophists. Oh, men of the West, who would play at being the Saviors of mankind before they even spare the life of a mosquito whose sting threatens them!, would you be partakers of Divine Wisdom or true Theosophists? Then do as the gods when incarnated do. Feel yourselves the vehicles of the whole humanity, mankind as part of yourselves, and act accordingly. * * * * * "

These are golden words; may you assimilate them! This is the hope of one who signs herself most sincerely the devoted sister *and servant* of every true follower of the Masters of Theosophy.

Yours fraternally,

H. P. Blavatsky

1890

Fourth Annual Convention — April 27–28
American Section of the Theosophical Society
Palmer House, Chicago, Illinois

Message delivered on behalf of H. P. Blavatsky
by Bertram Keightley, afternoon session, April 27

Reproduced verbatim from the printed
Report of Proceedings, pp. 27–30

The following cablegram was received by William Q. Judge just after adjournment:

LONDON, APRIL 26, 1890

JUDGE, GENERAL SECRETARY

GREETINGS TO CONVENTION. TOO SICK TO WRITE PERSONALLY.

H. P. BLAVATSKY

Message Communicated on Behalf of Madame H. P. Blavatsky by Bertram Keightley

I am directed by H. P. Blavatsky to read to you, as well as I can remember it, what she wished me to say to the Convention for her, as she has been too sick to write you her customary salutatory letter.

Brother Theosophists and Co-workers:

The new cycle which has opened for Theosophy is already beginning to bear fruit. The progress made by the movement during the last year is more marked than ever before, but, while encouraging us, it is also a reminder that the time of harvest is rapidly drawing nigh, soon to be followed by the winter with storms and tempests. Thus, though congratulating all of you, my earnest and active co-workers for our noble cause, and especially my dear colleague, Mr. W. Q. Judge, I must urge you to increase rather than relax your efforts.

Looking back over the past year, see how much has been accomplished by the power of union and unselfish devotion to work. During 1888–89 only six new Branches were formed in America; while in the past year fifteen additional Branches have been organized, while the numbers of the Society have increased even more rapidly in proportion. But even more important is the marked change of spirit among the members with regard to the Society and its work, of which signs are not wanting. The past twelve months have witnessed more activity in true Theosophical work, the endeavor to help others, than any preceding year in the history of the Society in the West. There are signs, visible though only gradually coming into sight, that its members are at last awakening from their apathy and setting to work in earnest to *practice* the first principle of true Theosophy — UNIVERSAL BROTHERHOOD. Gradually they are becoming alive to the duty of helping others, as they have been helped, by bringing a knowledge of the life-giving truths of Theosophy within the reach of all. The Tract Mailing Scheme is receiving increased support, more workers are volunteering assistance, and funds are forthcoming for carrying on the work with increased efficiency and ardor. The Pacific Coast Branches have set the example of undertaking this task as Branch work in a systematic and organized manner, and the elevation, the earnestness of the workers there deserve much praise. All gratitude is also due to the many faithful and earnest members in America who responded so nobly and generously to my appeal for aid to continue the publication of *Lucifer*. My heartiest thanks are theirs personally, one and all, and the fruit of their efforts will be seen in the future career of the magazine.

In England the past year has witnessed a rapid growth and a great extension of the Society and its work. Our cause has gained two noble and devoted adherents, whose names have been prominent for long years past in connection with every effort to bring real aid to suffering humanity — Annie Besant and Herbert Burrows. In them our movement in the West has gained able exponents both with pen and voice. They fill to some extent the long and sorely-felt need of speakers who could place Theosophy in its true light before large audiences, and I, especially, am deeply indebted to Annie Besant for her invaluable assistance and cooperation in the conduct of *Lucifer*.

New Branches have been formed here in the past twelve months, large numbers of members have joined our ranks, while the growth of general interest in Theosophy is evidenced by the changed tone of the Press and the frequent letters and articles on the subject of Theosophy. So great is the increase of interest in London that we find ourselves obliged to build a large meeting hall, at the new Headquarters to which we shall remove in August for the weekly meetings of the Blavatsky Lodge, as our old home is quite too small to accommodate the number of enquirers who attend the meetings.

Colonel Olcott's prolonged stay in England has been of great assistance to our work. His lectures throughout England and Ireland have been the cause of the formation of several new Branches, and his example and influence have done much good on all sides. To myself his presence has been a great pleasure and satisfaction, and the added strength when the "Two Founders" were once more side by side has made itself felt in every department of our work. It was with great regret that I saw him leave for India without paying his promised visit to America; but the Society in the East has most need of his presence, and the death of Mr. Powell rendered his direct return imperative. Though not personally acquainted with Mr. Powell, I cannot forbear paying a heartfelt tribute of gratitude to his memory for the splendid work he did for the Society, and for the nobility of his complete self-sacrifice to the service of Humanity. Colonel Olcott was accompanied on his return to India by two of our staff of workers here, Mr. Bowles Daly and Mr. E. D. Fawcett, whose presence at Adyar will, I trust, be of great value to my beloved colleague, our President-Founder.

A large part of these results is due to the added strength, and, above all, the increased spirit of solidarity, which the organization of the Esoteric Section has infused into the T.S. To the members of that Section I say: See and realize what great results can be achieved by those who are really in earnest and unite unselfishly to work for humanity. Let this year's outcome show you in unmistakable signs the weighty responsibility that rests upon you, not only towards the Society, but towards the whole of Humanity. Therefore do not for one moment relax in your efforts; press closer, shoulder to shoulder, every day; stand together as one man, come what may, fine weather or storm, and the victory of the cause to which you have pledged yourselves is certain. Striving thus in unison with your Higher Self, your efforts must and will be fruitful of good to the Society, to yourselves, to Humanity. Coming years will show a steady, healthy growth, a strong, united organization, a durable, reliable, and efficient instrument ready to the Masters' hands. Once united in real solidarity, in the true spirit of Universal Brotherhood, no power can overthrow you, no obstacle bar your progress, no barrier check the advance of Theosophy in the coming century.

But enough of the past. Let the encouragement we draw from a survey of the results accomplished in the year that has fled serve to spur us on to greater efforts and more strenuous exertions. Let it make all feel that there is a power behind the Society which will give us the strength we need, which will enable us to move the world, if we will but UNITE and WORK as one mind, one heart. The Masters require only that each shall do *his best*, and, above all, that each shall strive in reality to feel himself one with his fellow-workers. It is not a dull agreement on intellectual questions, or an impossible unanimity as to all details of work, that is needed; but a true, hearty, earnest devotion to our cause which will lead each to help his brother to the utmost of his power to *work* for that cause, whether or not we agree as to the exact method of carrying on that work. The only man who is absolutely wrong in his method is the one who *does nothing;* each can and should cooperate with all and all with each in a large-hearted spirit of comradeship to forward the work of bringing Theosophy home to every man and woman in the country.

Let us look forward, not backward. What of the coming year? And first a word of warning. As the preparation for the new cycle proceeds, as the forerunners of the new sub-race make their appearance on the American continent, the latent psychic and occult powers in man are beginning to germinate and grow. Hence the rapid growth of such movements as Christian Science, Mind Cure, Metaphysical Healing, Spiritual Healing, and so forth. All these movements represent nothing but different phases of the exercise of these growing powers — as yet not understood and therefore but too often ignorantly misused. Understand once for all that there is nothing "spiritual" or "divine" in *any* of these manifestations. The cures effected by them are due simply to the unconscious exercise of occult power on the *lower* planes of nature — usually of *prana* or life-currents. The conflicting theories of all these schools are based on misunderstood and misapplied metaphysics, often on grotesquely absurd logical fallacies. But the one feature common to most of them, a feature which presents the most danger in the near future, is this. In nearly every case, the tenor of the teachings of these schools is such as to lead people to regard the healing process as being applied to the *mind* of the patient. Here lies the danger, for any such process — however cunningly disguised in words and hidden by false noses — is simply to psychologize the patient. In other words, whenever the healer interferes — consciously or unconsciously — with the free mental action of the person he treats, it is — Black Magic. Already these so-called sciences of "Healing" are being used to gain a livelihood. Soon some sharp person will find out that by the same process the minds of others can be influenced in many directions, and the selfish motive of personal gain and money-getting having been once allowed to creep in, the one-time "healer" may be insensibly led on to use his power to acquire wealth or some other object of his desire.

This is one of the dangers of the new cycle, aggravated enormously by the pressure of competition and the struggle for existence. Happily new tendencies are also springing up, working to change the basis of men's daily lives from selfishness to altruism. The Nationalist Movement is an application of Theosophy.* But remember, all of you, that if Nationalism is an application of Theosophy, it is the latter which must ever stand first in your sight. Theosophy is indeed the life, the indwelling spirit which makes every true reform a vital reality, for Theosophy is Universal Brotherhood, the very foundation as well as the keystone of all movements toward the amelioration of our condition.

What I said last year remains true today, that is, that the Ethics of Theosophy are more important than any divulgement of psychic laws and facts. The latter relate wholly to the material and evanescent part of the septenary man, but the Ethics sink into and take hold of the real man — the reincarnating Ego. We are outwardly creatures of but a day; within we are eternal. Learn, then, well the doctrines of Karma and Reincarnation, and teach, practice, promulgate that system of life

---

[*In January 1888 Edward Bellamy published *Looking Backward, 2000–1887*, which envisioned a new order based on human brotherhood and the equality of all men, economically and socially. As a result, Nationalist Clubs were organized first at Boston, Mass., then across the country. These Clubs had the backing of theosophists, who saw in the Nationalist Movement a practical means to further their ideal of universal brotherhood. However, in 1890 when the Movement linked itself with politics it lost the support of theosophists, and in a few years its momentum had dissipated. See *Edward Bellamy* by Arthur E. Morgan, 1948, pp. 260–75; see also *The Key to Theosophy* by H. P. Blavatsky, pp. 44–5. — K. V. M.]

and thought which alone can save the coming races. Do not work merely for the Theosophical Society, but *through* it for Humanity.

May Theosophy grow more and more a living power in the lives of each one of our members, and may the coming year be yet more full of good work and healthy progress than the one just closing, is the wish of your humble co-worker and fellow member.

IV

1891

Fifth Annual Convention — April 26–27
American Section of the Theosophical Society
Steinert Hall, Boston, Massachusetts

Letter from H. P. Blavatsky read by
Annie Besant, afternoon session, April 26

Reproduced verbatim from the original typescript in the
Archives of the Theosophical Society, Pasadena

To the Boston Convention, T. S., 1891

For the third time since my return to Europe in 1885, I am able to send to my brethren in Theosophy and fellow citizens of the United States a delegate from England to attend the annual Theosophical Convention and speak by word of mouth my greeting and warm congratulations. Suffering in body as I am continually, the only consolation that remains to me is to hear of the progress of the Holy Cause to which my health and strength have been given; but to which, now that these are going, I can offer only my passionate devotion and never-weakening good wishes for its success and welfare. The news therefore that comes from America, mail after mail, telling of new Branches and of well-considered and patiently worked-out plans for the advancement of Theosophy cheers and gladdens me with its evidences of growth, more than words can tell. Fellow-Theosophists, I am proud of your noble work in the New World; Sisters and Brothers of America, I thank and I bless you for your unremitting labors for the common cause, so dear to us all.

Let me remind you all once more that such work is now more than ever needed. The period which we have now reached in the cycle that will close between 1897–8 is, and will continue to be, one of great conflict and continued strain. If the T. S. can hold through it, good; if not, while Theosophy will remain unscathed, the Society will perish – perchance most ingloriously – and the World will suffer. I fervently hope that I may not see such a disaster in my present body. The critical nature of the stage on which we have entered is as well known to the forces that fight against us as to those that fight on our side. No opportunity will be lost of sowing dissension, of taking advantage of mistaken and false moves, of instilling doubt, of augmenting difficulties, of breathing suspicions, so that by any and every means the unity of the Society may be broken and the ranks of our Fellows thinned and thrown into disarray. Never has it been more necessary for the Members of the T. S. to lay to heart the old parable of the bundle of sticks, than it is at the present time: divided, they will inevitably be broken, one by one; united, there is no force on Earth able to destroy our Brotherhood. Now I have marked with pain, a tendency among you, as among the Theosophists in Europe and India, to quarrel over trifles, and to allow your very devotion to the cause of Theosophy to lead you into disunion. Believe me, that apart from such natural tendency, owing to the inherent imperfections of Human Nature, advantage is often taken by our ever-watchful enemies of your noblest qualities to betray and to mislead you. Skeptics will laugh at this statement, and even some of you may put small faith in the actual existence of the terrible forces of these mental, hence subjective and invisible, yet withal living and potent, influences around all of us. But there they are, and I know of more than one among you who have felt them, and have actually been forced to acknowledge these extraneous mental pressures. On those of you who are unselfishly and sincerely devoted to the Cause, they will produce little, if any, impression. On some others, those who place their personal pride higher than their duty to the T. S., higher even than their Pledge to their divine SELF, the effect is generally disastrous. Self-watchfulness is never more necessary than when a personal wish to lead, and wounded vanity, dress themselves in the peacock's feathers of devotion and altruistic work; but at the present crisis of the Society a lack of self-control and watchfulness may become fatal in every case. But these diabolical attempts of our powerful enemies — the irreconcilable foes of the truths now being given out and practically asserted — may be frustrated. If every Fellow in the Society were content to be an impersonal force for good, careless of praise or blame so long as he subserved the purposes of the Brotherhood, the progress made would astonish the World and place the Ark of the T. S. out of danger. Take for your motto in conduct during the coming year, "Peace with All who love Truth in sincerity," and the Convention of 1892 will bear eloquent witness to the strength that is born of unity.

Your position as the forerunners of the sixth sub-race of the fifth root-race has its own special perils as well as its special advantages. Psychism, with all its allurements and all its dangers, is necessarily developing among you, and you must beware lest the Psychic outruns the Manasic and Spiritual development. Psychic capacities held perfectly under control, checked and directed by the Manasic principle, are valuable aids in development. But these capacities running riot, controlling instead of controlled, using instead of being used, lead the Student into the most dangerous delusions and the certainty of moral destruction. Watch therefore carefully this development, inevitable in your race and evolution-period, so that it may finally work for good and not for evil; and receive, in advance, the sincere and potent blessings of Those whose goodwill will never fail you, if you do not fail yourselves.

Here in England I am glad to be able to report to you that steady and rapid progress is being made. Annie Besant will give you details of our work, and will tell you of the growing strength and influence of our Society; the reports which she bears from the European and British Sections speak for themselves in their record of activities. The English character, difficult to reach, but solid and tenacious when once aroused, adds to our Society a valuable factor, and there are being laid in England strong and firm foundations for the T. S. of the twentieth Century. Here, as with you, attempts are being successfully made to bring to bear the influence of Hindu on English thought, and many of our Hindu brethren are now writing for *Lucifer* short and clear papers on Indian philosophies. As it is one of the tasks of the T. S. to draw together the East and the West, so that each may supply the qualities lacking in the other, and develop more fraternal feelings among Nations so various, this literary intercourse, will, I hope, prove of the utmost service in Aryanizing Western thought.

The mention of *Lucifer* reminds me that the now assured position of that magazine is very largely due to the help rendered at a critical moment by the American Fellows. As my one absolutely unfettered

better than I can write them. After all, every wish and thought I can utter are summed up in this one sentence, the never dormant wish of my heart, "Be Theosophists, Work for Theosophy!" — Theosophy first, and Theosophy last; for its practical realisation alone can save the Western World from that selfish and unbrotherly feeling that now divides race from race, one nation from the other, and from that hatred of class and social strifes, that are the curse and disgrace of so-called Christian peoples. Theosophy alone can save it from sinking entirely into that mere luxurious materialism in which it will decay and putrify as older civilisations have done. In your hands, Brothers, is placed in trust the welfare of the coming century: and great as is the trust, so great is also the responsibility. My own span of life may not be long, and if any of you have learned aught from my xx-teachings, or have gained by my help a glimpse of the True Light, I ask you in return, to strenghten the cause by the triumph of which, that True Light, made still brigter and more glorious through your indivi-

ety secured.

May the blessings of the past and present great Teachers rest upon you. From myself accept collectively, the assurance of my true, never-wavering fraternal feelings, and the sincere heart-felt thanks for the work done by all the workers,

From their Servant to the last,

H. P. Blavatsky

H. P. BLAVATSKY.

medium of communication with Theosophists all over the World, its continuance was of grave importance to the whole Society. In its pages, month by month, I give such public teaching as is possible on Theosophical doctrines, and so carry on the most important of our Theosophical work. The magazine now just covers its expenses, and if Lodges and individual Fellows would help in increasing its circulation, it would become more widely useful than it is at the present time. Therefore, while thanking from the bottom of my heart all those who so generously helped to place the magazine on a solid foundation, I should be glad to see a larger increase in the number of regular subscribers, for I regard these as my pupils, among whom I shall find some who will show the capacity for receiving further instruction.

And now I have said all; I am not sufficiently strong to write you a more lengthy message, and there is the less need for me to do so, as my friend and trusted messenger, Annie Besant, she who is my right arm here, will be able to explain to you my wishes more fully and better than I can write them. After all, every wish and thought I can utter are summed up in this one sentence, the never dormant wish of my heart, "Be Theosophists, Work for Theosophy!" — Theosophy first, and Theosophy last; for its *practical* realization alone can save the Western World from that selfish and unbrotherly feeling that now divides race from race, one nation from the other, and from that hatred of class and [from] social strifes,* that are the curse and disgrace of so-called Christian peoples. Theosophy alone can save it from sinking entirely into that mere luxurious materialism in which it will decay and putrefy as older civilizations have done. In your hands, Brothers, is placed in trust the welfare of the coming century: and great as is the trust, so great is also the responsibility. My own span of life may not be long, and if any of you have learned aught from my teachings, or have gained by my help a glimpse of the True Light, I ask you in return, to strengthen the cause by the triumph of which, that True Light, made still brighter and more glorious through your individual and collective efforts, will lighten the World, and thus to let me see,

---

[*The word "strifes" was changed to "considerations" in the printed "Report of Proceedings." — K. V. M.]

before I part with this worn-out body, the stability of the Society secured.

May the blessings of the past and present great Teachers rest upon you. From myself accept collectively, the assurance of my true, never-wavering fraternal feelings, and the sincere heartfelt thanks for the work done by all the workers,

From their Servant to the last,

H. P. BLAVATSKY

V

1891

Fifth Annual Convention — April 26–27
American Section of the Theosophical Society
Steinert Hall, Boston, Massachusetts

Letter from H. P. Blavatsky, dated April 15, 1891,
read by Annie Besant, afternoon session, April 26

Reproduced verbatim from the original in the
handwriting of G. R. S. Mead, except for
the closing salutation and signature, held in the
Archives of the Theosophical Society, Pasadena

Theosophical Society: European Section

> 19, Avenue Road,
> Regent's Park,
> London, N.W. 15:4:1891

To the Vth Convention of the American Section
of the Theosophical Society

Brother Theosophists: —

I have purposely omitted any mention of my oldest friend and fellow-worker, W. Q. Judge, in my general address to you, because I think that his unflagging and self-sacrificing efforts for the building up of Theosophy in America deserve special mention.

Had it not been for W. Q. Judge, Theosophy would not be where it is today in the United States. It is he who has mainly built up the movement among you, and he who has proved in a thousand ways his entire loyalty to the best interests of Theosophy and the Society.

Mutual admiration should play no part in a Theosophical Convention, but honor should be given where honor is due, and I gladly take this opportunity of stating in public, by the mouth of my friend and colleague, Annie Besant, my deep appreciation of the work of your General Secretary, and of publicly tendering him my most sincere thanks and deeply-felt gratitude, in the name of Theosophy, for the noble work he is doing and has done.

Yours fraternally,

H. P. Blavatsky

Historical Perspective

All books and magazines quoted, and all letters and documents not specifically referenced herein, are held in the Archives of the Theosophical Society, Pasadena, California.

Historical Perspective

Kirby Van Mater

ALMOST A CENTURY has passed since H. P. Blavatsky sent her letters to the American Conventions. They remain significant for us today, although both the world and the structure of the theosophical effort have altered considerably. While we each can apply her statements to our individual situation, it may be helpful to look briefly at the general context which drew them forth, keeping in mind several of the important currents which developed after her public work began.

Mme. Blavatsky's theosophical endeavors seem to fall into three periods: America, 1873–1878; India, 1879–1885; and Europe, 1885 until her death in 1891. The first of these began in July 1873 when, on orders from her teacher, she came to the United States from Paris. Initially, she sought to interest members of the Spiritualist movement in the philosophy and meaning behind their phenomena but, as this proved a failure, in July 1875 she was told "to establish a philosophico-religious Society & choose a name for it — also to choose Olcott [to head it]."[1] As a consequence, in September H. P. Blavatsky with Henry S. Olcott, William Q. Judge, and thirteen others, founded the Theosophical Society in New York City, with President Olcott giving the inaugural address at its first official meeting on November 17, 1875.

The aims and objectives set forth in the Society's preamble and bylaws were not so defined as they were later to become. Basically the members sought "to collect and diffuse a knowledge of the laws

---

[1] H. P. Blavatsky's "Scrap Book," quoted in *The Golden Book of the Theosophical Society*, p. 19.

which govern the universe," and to investigate all philosophies, religions, and sciences. They advocated unselfish devotion, courage, and purity of life and thought in the search for truth. In considering the qualifications of applicants for fellowship, the Society made no distinction of race, sex, color, country, or creed.[2]

In September 1875, while in Ithaca, New York, as the guest of Professor Hiram Corson, Mme. Blavatsky commenced the writing of *Isis Unveiled*. She wrote almost continuously and by 1877 had completed this large two-volume work, in which she was assisted editorially by Colonel Olcott and Dr. Alexander Wilder owing to her lack of fluency in English. Her chief purposes, aside from attacking dogma and materialism in both science and religion, were to restore to man the lost knowledge that he was essentially a spiritual being, and to point to the existence of an ancient wisdom known to all peoples in all ages. When the contract with her New York publisher was signed, she told W. Q. Judge: "Now I must go to India." She had always said she would leave for India as soon as *Isis* was finished and the Society under way, but this did not come to pass until the close of the next year.

Throughout this period the goals of the Theosophical Society were being clarified, as shown by the one-page statement issued by President Olcott in May 1878. This read in part:

> The Society teaches and expects its fellows to personally exemplify the highest morality and religious aspiration; to oppose the materialism of science and every form of dogmatic theology . . . ; to make known among Western nations the long-suppressed *facts* about Oriental religious philosophies, their ethics, chronology, esoterism, symbolism; . . . to disseminate a knowledge of the sublime teachings of that pure esoteric system of the archaic period . . . ; finally, and chiefly, to aid in the institution of a Brotherhood of Humanity, wherein all good and pure men, of every race, shall recognize each other as the equal effects (upon this planet) of one Uncreate, Universal, Infinite, and Everlasting Cause.[3]

---

[2] *Preamble and By-laws of the Theosophical Society*, October 30, 1875; on this date Henry S. Olcott was elected President; H. P. Blavatsky, Corresponding Secretary; and William Q. Judge, Counsel to the Society.

[3] *The Theosophical Society: Its Origin, Plan and Aims.*

In December 1878 H. P. Blavatsky and Colonel Olcott set sail for England en route to India, leaving behind a relatively small membership to forward the work of the Theosophical Society. General Abner Doubleday was appointed President ad interim and William Q. Judge was made Recording Secretary. But the Society in America did not grow much during the next several years. Correspondence with India took many months, and General Doubleday felt unprepared and uninformed for the task that was his. As he later wrote to Dr. Elliott Coues:

> I will now give you in brief my own statement concerning the N.Y. Branch.
> When H.P.B. went away she asked me to act as President of the N.Y. Branch. I was much astonished at the request for I was merely an inquirer, had but recently joined the society and was very imperfectly acquainted with the subject. At that time I was not busily engaged at anything. All the others were too much occupied in getting a livelihood to pay proper attention to Theos. Judge who had been connected with H.P.B. and Olcott from the beginning was the proper person to take charge of it. But he was in great straits at the time to know how he should support his family. Wilder & Weisse were Vice Presidents. It was arranged that for the time being meetings of the society would be dispensed with and all business would be managed by a council, consisting of Doubleday, Wilder, Weisse & Curtis (The newspaper reporter) Judge was corresponding secrt. and Maynard Treas.
> I accepted the position at the earnest request of H.P.B., intending to rely principally on Judge for counsel and assistance; but Judge thought he had found a mining locality in Venezuela where many valuable leads could be easily worked. He went to Campana Venez. leaving me ignorant and inexperienced as I was to run the society, without knowing anything of the individuals, that composed it. . . .
> I never could get more than a half a dozen members together to attend a meeting. Judge was constantly absent. His brother dropped us. Maynard got offended & left. Wilder resigned from poverty. Weisse resigned. The Brooklyn members would not come to N.Y. without a specific statement of what I supposed [proposed] to have done at the meetings. Then we were detained 2 years waiting for a *ritual*, which Olcott said we must have. . . .

I suppose all this delay is for the best and these obstacles may have been purposely thrown in our way. . . .[4]

In India, however, there was considerable response to Theosophy and a great deal to be done. Mme. Blavatsky and Colonel Olcott traveled up and down India, and received visitors often till late at night — scholars, leaders of religious and various other societies, as well as inquirers. They carried on a wide correspondence which soon became too heavy to handle individually. As a consequence, they founded *The Theosophist* in October 1879, not only to meet the demand for a more comprehensive exposition of the ancient wisdom, but also to be a forum for scholars of the world's philosophical and religious beliefs. The magazine was conducted by Mme. Blavatsky and its circulation throughout the world shortly reached such proportions that it began to pay its way.

It should be mentioned that several months before Mme. Blavatsky and Colonel Olcott left the United States, the Theosophical Society had linked itself to the "Arya-Samaj of Arya-wart," a new and fast-growing movement in India whose stated principles and aims were close to those of the Theosophical Society. Olcott and H.P.B., as she became known, worked within this structure until 1882 when they were forced to strike off on their own due to the narrowing views entertained by its leader, Swami Dya Nand Saraswati, towards those philosophies and religions not based on the Vedas. Since the theosophists from America fraternized with all peoples, they were accepted by the native population, and several Indian philosophical and literary

---

[4] Report sent to Elliott Coues by Abner Doubleday; it is undated, but probably written in 1885 as Professor Coues became President of the American Board of Control of the T.S. in July of that year (see below, p. 59).

General Doubleday joined the Theosophical Society soon after it had been founded, and unswervingly supported its work until his death in 1893.

Alexander Wilder, M.D., Platonic scholar and author, was commissioned by J. W. Bouton, publisher, to edit *Isis Unveiled*. As a result, he became a personal friend of H. P. Blavatsky and joined the Society in 1876. The "resignation" referred to by General Doubleday concerned only Dr. Wilder's appointment in 1879 as Vice President of the Society. He felt that the Society should have a more efficient officer to promote its cause. He remained an active member until the turn of the century.

HISTORICAL PERSPECTIVE 51

bodies became affiliated with the Theosophical Society.[5] They were, on the other hand, viewed with dismay by the Anglo-Indian community, particularly by the missionary element.

It is not our intent to give here a complete outline of the many activities in Asia or to trace all the effects of H.P.B.'s and Olcott's endeavors. It is noteworthy, however, that from February 1879 to January 1883, 39 Branches were established in India and Ceylon (Sri Lanka), while only six were in existence in the rest of the world; and 46 new charters were issued in India and Ceylon in 1883 alone, with only a half dozen new Branches chartered in the rest of the world. For the revival of Sanskrit learning and general education, schools and Sanskrit classes were started for boys and girls and also adults, 27 schools being in operation in India by the close of 1883, with another three schools and one college for teaching Sanskrit scheduled to be opened that year. The work in Ceylon is perhaps the most dramatic symbol of the impact of the theosophical influence in Asia. With the help of the Theosophical Society, principally the labors of Henry S. Olcott, the Singhalese Buddhists obtained religious and educational freedom, and their faith took on new stature and meaning in their own eyes and in the eyes of the world.

The bylaws and objectives of the T. S. underwent various modifications in India, slowly arriving at a simple and broad expression reflecting the growing understanding of the membership. As early as 1879 the printed rules were headed "The Theosophical Society or Universal Brotherhood," and by 1882 there were three declared objects: "*First.* — to form the nucleus of a Universal Brotherhood of Humanity, without distinction of race, creed or colour. *Second.* — to promote the

---

[5] H. P. Blavatsky to A. B. Griggs, February 16, 1881, copy in Doubleday Notebook, no. 8, p. 104; see also *A Report of the Sixth Anniversary of the Theosophical Society*, Bombay, January 12, 1882; p. 6.

On March 7, 1879, just three weeks after their arrival in India, Mme. Blavatsky and Colonel Olcott rented a small house in the center of Bombay at 108, Girgaum Back Road. This served as headquarters for their theosophical and editorial activities until December 1880, when they moved to a more spacious bungalow, "The Crow's Nest," at Breach Candy on the outskirts of Bombay. Here they remained until December 1882 when a formal headquarters for the Theosophical Society was established at Adyar, Madras.

study of Aryan and other Eastern literature, religions and sciences and vindicate its importance. *Third.* — to investigate the hidden mysteries of Nature and the Psychical powers latent in man."[6]

Perhaps one of the most significant events of that time was the association with A. P. Sinnett, editor of *The Pioneer*, an influential newspaper at Allahabad. Having heard of *Isis Unveiled* and wishing very much to meet its author, he entered into correspondence with Mme. Blavatsky and Colonel Olcott shortly after their arrival in India in February 1879. In December Mr. and Mrs. Sinnett invited the travelers to visit their summer home in Simla, at which time they made the acquaintance of several persons of note, among whom was A. O. Hume, British Civil Servant. During a subsequent visit in the fall of 1880, the now well-known correspondence between Sinnett and Hume and the Masters K.H. and M. was begun.[7] Because of the great interest of Hume and Sinnett in psychic matters H. P. Blavatsky produced a good deal of phenomena for their benefit. From these experiences as well as from the letters they received from the Masters, Sinnett composed his first book, *The Occult World*, published in 1881. A second work, *Esoteric Buddhism*, appearing in 1883, was based on further correspondence with the Mahatmas; in this volume he gave his view of theosophy with respect to the history and relation of man and universe. These two books immediately produced a great stir in the Western world. Grateful, however, as the Adepts were for these publications, they were not entirely pleased with Sinnett's accent in *The Occult World* on the "Brothers" and on phenomena, or with certain mistaken notions concerning the philosophy in *Esoteric Buddhism*.[8] Moreover, the popularity of these works and the occult philosophy they expounded, coupled with the evident success of the Theosophical Society throughout India, intensified the growing antagonism of the missionaries, creating a climate which led eventually to their attack on H. P. Blavatsky in *The Christian College Magazine*.

The year 1884 brought calamity and change to the Theosophical

---

[6] Ibid., p. 11.
[7] Published in 1923 under the title, *The Mahatma Letters to A. P. Sinnett*, compiled and edited by A. Trevor Barker.
[8] See *The Mahatma Letters to A. P. Sinnett*, pp. 227, 292, 323, 356, 364.

Society. It was determined that Colonel Olcott would travel to England to resolve the differences in the London Lodge between its president, Dr. Anna Kingsford, and Mr. Sinnett, and at the same time he would take up with the British government certain vital religious and educational matters on behalf of the Buddhists of Ceylon. At the last moment it was decided that H.P.B. would travel with him to Europe. They left Bombay for Marseilles on February 20, not to return until the end of the year. During their absence from Adyar, M. and Mme. Coulomb, members of the household staff, conspired to discredit Mme. Blavatsky. Unable to blackmail members at Headquarters in charge of theosophical affairs by threatening to make public certain statements which would seem to deny the existence of H.P.B.'s teachers and the authenticity of the phenomena she produced, the Coulombs turned to the Christian missionaries. Later, on September 11, 1884, *The Christian College Magazine* printed a vicious story based on statements and forged documents supplied by the Coulombs, who claimed that H. P. Blavatsky was fraudulent not only in producing phenomena but also in writing letters in the name of the Mahatmas.

It is interesting to note that Judge was in India at the time these charges were published. The start of his journey there had coincided with H.P.B.'s and Olcott's trip to Europe so that the three co-founders met in Paris at the end of March. Judge stayed with them about three months, participating closely in all that went on, even to writing, at H.P.B.'s request, a chapter on elementals for the projected *Secret Doctrine* (though, he tells us later, it was not used). Toward the end of June he continued on to India, armed with documents from Olcott to act in the name of the President in all matters concerning the Headquarters and, if he deemed it advisable, to abolish the Board of Control at Adyar.[9] But Judge did not stay there more than a few months, scarcely long enough to effect any noticeable change in the basic situation at Adyar. On his return from India he dedicated his full energies toward building up the work in America.

---

[9] The Board of Control was a Headquarters Executive Committee appointed by special order of President Olcott to have jurisdiction over financial, executive, and supervisory affairs of the Society while he was away in Europe (see *Supplement to The Theosophist*, February and March, 1884).

Meanwhile, Mme. Blavatsky had returned to Madras in December. Immediately she declared her intention to go to court against her accusers, but despite her fervent pleas she was prevented from doing so by Colonel Olcott. Writing several years later in defense of H. P. Blavatsky, Olcott explains:

> Much has been made out of the fact that she did not go into Court to vindicate her character against the palpable libels of the Missionary and allied parties. For this *she is not to blame:* quite the contrary. But for my vehement protests she would have dragged the adversaries into the Madras Courts as soon as she got back from London, *via* Cairo, in 1884. A friend had offered her Rs. 10,000 to cover the expenses. It was then barely a fortnight before the time for the Annual Convention of our Society — December 27th, 1884 — and I insisted upon her waiting until a Special Judicial Committee of the Convention should advise her as to her proper course. We were — I told her — the property of the Society, and bound to sink our private preferences and selves for the public good. She was stubborn to that degree, that I *had to threaten to quit my official position* before she would listen to reason. The Convention met, and the case was referred to a Committee composed of Hindu Judges and other legal gentlemen of high official and private standing. They unanimously reported against H.P.B.'s going to law; . . .[10]

At the same time a young man by the name of Richard Hodgson arrived at Adyar, sent from London by the Society for Psychical Research (SPR), to investigate the accusations against H. P. Blavatsky. A year later the committee appointed to study his findings identified her as "one of the most accomplished, ingenious, and interesting impostors in history."[11] Olcott continues:

> On the very day when the charges against her were first published in the *Times*, she — then in London — wrote that paper an indignant denial. I have seen no proof since then to support the contrary. The alleged

---

[10] "H. P. B.'s Departure," *Lucifer*, August 1891, p. 447.
[11] *Proceedings of the Society for Psychical Research*, December 1885, p. 207; see also Charles J. Ryan's *H. P. Blavatsky and the Theosophical Movement*, ch. 13; and *Obituary: The "Hodgson Report" on Madame Blavatsky* by Adlai E. Waterman.

letters to Mme. Coulomb were never shown her or me; the Coulombs stand self-impeached as to honesty of character; Mr. Hodgson's report evinces his dense ignorance at the time of psychical and mediumistic laws and the indispensable rules of spiritualistic research, even of the commonest rules of legal evidence; . . .[12]

The Coulomb-Missionary attack upon H.P.B. and the added pressure placed upon her in not being permitted to defend the honor of her teachers broke down her always precarious health. Companions and friends despaired for her life, and her doctor urged that she leave India at once for a more equable climate as the only possible chance of her staying alive. In September, after the accusations had appeared in the Madras paper, Mme. Blavatsky, then in Elberfeld, Germany, had handed in her resignation as Corresponding Secretary, but was persuaded to withdraw it "at the urgent request and solicitation of Society friends." Nonetheless, the next spring on March 21 she tendered it again, and this time it was accepted, and she departed from India ten days later, never to return to that land.[13] She was to all purposes alone, left to recover her health in Europe, if she could. In the eyes of the world she was leaving the arena to her accusers, offering no defense against their charges.

H.P.B.'s own feelings are clearly portrayed in her letter of April 11, 1885, written to Olcott on board the S.S. *Pehio* [*Pei Ho*], near Aden:

> Where to, what for, I am going away I do not know unto this day. Of course we will stop somewhere near Naples — and what next? What shall I do with H. [Franz Hartmann]? How shall we live. If I have strength I will write for the Russian papers — and if I have none left? Have you sent me to die far away or to . . . [word illegible] and come back. If the former, then say so, and I will know what to do; if the latter then how under what circumstances what is it *that must happen* that I should come back home. For mind you, I do not suppose that you would allow people to believe that the Society has sent me away,

---

[12] *Lucifer*, August 1891, p. 447. It should be remembered that Colonel Olcott was a lawyer by profession and that during the Civil War he was appointed Special Commissioner of the War Department (U.S.A.) with the responsibility to unearth fraud committed by contractors against the government.

[13] *Supplement to The Theosophist*, May 1885, p. 195.

dismissed me as a tricky butler, as a Coulomb, for it is *just that* the Coulombs and padris wanted. They have clamoured for it, printed it, and published that wish, saying publicly that the Society was "bound to expel me," etc. Is it that wish you have intended accomplishing? I hope *for your and the Society's sake* it is not so. For Master told me most plainly that if the Society did not recall me before 1886, They would retire entirely from any connection with it; signify so to the L.L. [London Lodge] and other European and American Societies and break every connection with every member. THEY will not countenance ingratitude, Olcott, however guilty I may appear in the eyes of fools or even wise men for the matter of that. THEY DO EXIST – phenomena or no phenomena; but as "Benjamin" [Djual Kul] remarked – I am the only one, for the present, in full possession of their doctrines and ready to give out of it as much as I can. After me comes Subba Row who knows more than I do, but who will not give out a tittle of it in its true light not for a kingdom. It is the Society that needs *me* while I can do perfectly without it. But the question is not one of interest but of JUSTICE and Pride. It is not selfishness or personal pride, but I was sent by Them and whatever my failure I am Their agent: in insulting me the Society insults Them – that's all. Well, let it try the sad experiment . . .[14]

H. P. Blavatsky's coming to Europe in 1885 marks the opening of the final stage of her mission. In the years that followed she was to produce most of her literary works and establish a strong Society in the West – she in Europe and Judge in America. But there is an overlapping in all cycles: while the vitality in the old period is waning, there is a continuing of essential activity under a fresh impetus into the new time. In answer to the need for a more comprehensive discourse on theosophical doctrine than that found scattered throughout the pages of *Isis Unveiled* and in *The Theosophist*, an advertisement had appeared as early as the January 1884 *Supplement* to that magazine, stating that a recasting of *Isis Unveiled* called *The Secret Doctrine* would be issued in installments. H. P. Blavatsky had already commenced work on the manuscript at Adyar and had continued her writing after she went to Europe in the spring of 1884. The following January when she was

---

[14] *The Theosophist*, March 1925, pp. 784–5.

again in India she received from her teacher "the plan" for *The Secret Doctrine*, and although she labored constantly, the volumes were not published until 1888. It was only after Countess Wachtmeister joined Mme. Blavatsky in Würzburg in December 1885, to become her companion and look after all the affairs of running the household, that it was possible for H.P.B. to make real progress with her task. She then could write from early morning till evening. The Countess protected her friend in all possible ways and copied for her the corrected manuscripts in legible handwriting. They moved from Würzburg to Ostend in May 1886, with a number of delays en route, to continue working again on the manuscript.

Early in 1887, Bertram Keightley and then later Archibald, his nephew, traveled to Ostend to visit H.P.B. Representing a small group of members of the London Lodge who felt that the public work there needed a new impulse, they urged her to come to England, which she agreed to do if adequate lodging could be furnished. Soon, however, she became grievously ill and death was imminent. But to the amazement of her doctor and friends she recovered, and the Keightleys came again to make final arrangements for the move across the channel. In May she made her way by boat and train to the home of Mrs. Mabel Cook, known to many as Mabel Collins,[15] in Maycot, London. Here, with the help of several young members, the final preparation of *The Secret Doctrine* was begun. On the 28th of the same month Bertram Keightley wrote to Judge:

> H.P.B. is fairly well & working away right hard at the Secret Doctrine; which is *awfully good* & I am sure you will be immensely pleased with it. Tho' I date this from Linden Gardens, I am staying with HPB at Maycot, Crown Hill, Upper Norwood, S.E. where I expect she will be for the next two or three months. We have got a scheme on foot for establishing HPB in *winter* quarters near London where she can live in peace & gather the real workers in the Society around her. But whether it will succeed or even ever be really begun I cannot tell. All I know is that we shall do our level best to bring it about. Still do *not mention* anything about it; as "there's many a slip twixt the cup and

---

[15] Author of *Light on the Path, Through the Gates of Gold*, and other works.

the lip" & these things are best kept quiet till actually done. Anyway we mean a real effort to put new life into this dull L.L. [London Lodge] & the new Magazine, as the first step. The title at present in favour is "*Lucifer: the Lightbearer*," but no final decision has yet been come to. At any rate we *mean to do two things:* to make HPB as comfortable as we can & to prove to her that there are some at least who really appreciate her ceaseless self sacrifice & untiring exertions for the Cause.

The proposed move from Maycot to 17 Lansdowne Road and the first issue of *Lucifer* were realized in September. A year later, on November 1, 1888, *The Secret Doctrine* was published simultaneously in England and America.

In the early years there were those members in the Theosophical Society who dedicated the finest quality of their lives to the furtherance of its objectives and upon whose devoted labors its very life depended. A few at times acted from motives reflecting a confused concept of its aims and purposes, and these particular actions occasionally brought about grave stress within the Society. As the sensitive heart of the "Work," H. P. Blavatsky was compelled to act in order to protect the T. S., just as she responded in gratitude to those who comprehended its true mission.

During these years of Mme. Blavatsky's retirement from direct participation in theosophical affairs (1885–87), the Society had drifted away from the influence of the Adepts. This is apparent from a conversation she had with one of her teachers where he remarked that Colonel Olcott in spite of his great labors had during this time allowed the T. S. to liberate itself from their influence, and that it would not long survive his death.[16] Though the date of this discussion is not given, it can be placed approximately in the closing months of 1887 or early 1888. From this time onward till her death in 1891, H. P. Blavatsky played an increasingly significant role in the Society's administration so as to reestablish and maintain the work along the original lines. This caused some unhappiness and misunderstanding between herself and Colonel Olcott. Eventually, in 1890, much distressed over circumstances, he stated that he would resign as president at the next

---

[16] Cf. *Letters from the Masters of the Wisdom*, First Series, Letter 47, 5th edition.

convention in December. However, at the final moment he announced a change of mind and retained his position in the Society, though his views and lack of confidence in H.P.B.'s methods of work remained unchanged.

The serious situation that had arisen, due to the inner spirit of the work having been neglected, now faced H. P. Blavatsky with the challenge of having to reorient the attitude of the membership. The next four years, May 1887 to May 1891, were a period of renewal for the theosophical cause. There were but few strong centers outside of Asia when she left India in 1885, but by the closing months of 1890 the West under her stimulus had awakened and become the most active sector of the Society.

The reorganization and expansion of theosophical work in the United Kingdom as well as on the Continent were paralleled and in some respects foreshadowed in America under the direction of William Q. Judge. An American Board of Control had been established on May 13, 1884, by special order of President Olcott, while Judge on his way to India was staying with Mme. Blavatsky and Colonel Olcott in Paris. The Board was formed to guide the work and handle local problems for the membership in the United States; also to initiate new members and to grant temporary charters for new Branches without reference to the central Headquarters. It functioned in this capacity for two years, until June 6, 1886, when President Olcott, at the urging of Judge and H.P.B., requested that the American Board of Control be abolished. Instead, a Section of the Society, to be known as the American Section of the General Council of the Theosophical Society, was formed. The new organization was brought into being at a convention of all lodges held at Cincinnati, Ohio, on October 30–31, with Judge made General Secretary and Treasurer. On April 24, 1887, the first Convention of the American Section was held in New York, when a constitution and bylaws were adopted and adherence to the General Council declared, with Judge again elected General Secretary for the ensuing year.

All the trials of establishing a workable Section of the Theosophical Society thousands of miles from Headquarters were gone through by Judge in New York and the staff at Adyar. To multiply problems,

Olcott was away on theosophical affairs for extended periods and not always available for final decisions. Judge's eagerness to push ahead with the work in America, coupled with the continuing delays at Headquarters, caused a strain between him and Olcott, a condition which time did not ease. Judge's letter to Colonel Olcott of July 24, 1888, is revealing of the frustration felt by many Western theosophists, particularly officials, toward Headquarters in India:

> It is significant that the T.S. was started here [in the U.S.]. India is necessary to it, as I said in Path, & it to India. But India cannot claim to be it all. Indeed it is getting to be secondary I think, even if the Adepts still reside there. I am fully in accord with you as to the importance of the Library and all the rest, but I want to suggest that the T.S. if it is what it claims, a thing of ∴ creation, cannot remain where it was when it was started or where it got to in 1884. It must press on, and it must change or — it must die. Hence a change is expected in its 14th year which is heralded & felt to begin in its 13th. This is the 13th year and this will witness a change. I do not know if you are ready to meet it. It has seemed to me that you have of late got a fondness for forms; & I have always thought that you *gave away* your power to Boards & committees too much. Your idea that the T.S. must be put into such a shape that it might live on after your death is based upon the assumption that you are the only man who could carry it on and that at your death it would die unless its rules & constitution were fixed. This I do not concur in. If you died, some others would be provided. The T.S. is getting stuck and it has to be got out of the rut. Of course these are only my opinions.[17]

With the expansion of the work in Europe the difficulties between the Adyar Headquarters and the West were compounded. The next month on August 16 Judge wrote Archibald Keightley that as Olcott wished Europe to have an organization like that in America, Keightley ought to call a convention and make H.P.B. president of the new Section.[18] Though the European Section was not formed until 1890, a British Sec-

---

[17] Cf. *Practical Occultism: From the Private Letters of William Q. Judge*, pp. 109–10.
[18] Ibid., p. 112.

HISTORICAL PERSPECTIVE   61

tion was established in December 1888 with the aid of President Olcott who had been in London that fall.

The most telling step taken by Mme. Blavatsky at this time to bring the work of the Society into harmony with the original purposes was the organization of a formal Esoteric Section, although the Esoteric School — a relationship of disciples to Adepts — had existed since ancient times, and its influence was evident in the T. S. from the beginning. There had always been a desire on the part of the sincere students to come closer to the Mahatmas, and in 1883 H. P. Blavatsky wrote an informative article titled "Chelas and Lay Chelas," which included these comments:

> For centuries the selection of Chelas — outside the hereditary group within the *gon-pa* (temple) — has been made by the Himalayan Mahatmas themselves from among the class — in Tibet, a considerable one as to number — of natural mystics. The only exceptions have been in the cases of Western men like Fludd, Thomas Vaughan, Paracelsus, Pico di Mirandola, Count St. Germain, etc., whose temperamental affinity to this celestial science more or less forced the distant Adepts to come into personal relations with them, and enabled them to get such small (or large) proportion of the whole truth as was possible under their social surroundings. . . .
>
> But since the advent of the Theosophical Society, one of whose arduous tasks it was to reawaken in the Aryan mind the dormant memory of the existence of this science and of those transcendent human capabilities, the rules of Chela selection have become slightly relaxed in one respect. Many members of the Society becoming convinced by practical proof upon the above points, and rightly enough thinking that if other men had hitherto reached the goal, they too if inherently fitted, might reach it by following the same path, pressed to be taken as candidates. And as it would be an interference with Karma to deny them the chance of at least beginning — since they were so importunate, they were given it. The results have been far from encouraging so far, and it is to show these unfortunates the cause of their failure as much as to warn others against rushing heedlessly upon a similar fate, that the writing of the present article has been ordered. The candidates in question, though plainly warned against it in advance, began wrong by selfishly looking to the future and losing sight of the

past. They forgot that they had done nothing to deserve the rare honour of selection, nothing which warranted their expecting such a privilege; . . .[19]

The next year, in 1884, members of the London Lodge petitioned the Mahatmas to form an "Inner Group," and were granted permission to do so, but it did not last.[20] Again, in 1887 Judge wrote H. P. Blavatsky asking if esoteric studies might not be established in answer to requests he had received. He enclosed a suggested directive and formalities for her to use as she saw fit. She replied that he might go ahead without any document and that soon she would do something else. In 1888 she invited him to come to London to help her lay the foundation for this work.

Mme. Blavatsky wrote Olcott that same year concerning the plan for the formation of the Esoteric Section. As there was some difficulty with the Isis Branch in Paris, on August 7 he embarked for London on the S.S. *Shannon* in order to confer with her on these and other matters. He later wrote Judge that he had received a letter from K.H. while on board ship, the day before reaching Brindisi. This letter is informative as to the relationship of the Masters to H.P.B. and to Olcott:

> Again, as you approach London I have a word or two to say to you. Your impressibility is so changeful that I must not wholly depend upon it at this critical time. Of course you know that things were so brought to a focus as to necessitate the present journey and that the inspiration to make it came to you and to permit it to the Councillors *from without*. Put all needed restraint upon your feelings, so that you may do the right thing in this Western imbroglio. Watch your first impressions. The mistakes you make spring from failure to do this. Let neither your personal predilections, affections, suspicions nor antipathies affect your action.
>
> Misunderstandings have grown up between Fellows both in London and Paris, which imperil the interests of the movement. You will be told that the chief originator of most, if not of all these disturbances is H. P. B. This is not so; though her presence in England has, of course,

---

[19] *Supplement to The Theosophist,* July 1883, p. 10.
[20] Cf. *H. P. Blavatsky: Collected Writings,* vol. 6, pp. 250-4.

HISTORICAL PERSPECTIVE 63

a share in them. But the largest share rests with others, whose serene unconsciousness of their own defects is very marked and much to be blamed. One of the most valuable effects of Upasika's mission is that it drives men to self-study and destroys in them blind servility for persons.[21] Observe your own case, for example. But your revolt, good friend, against her infallibility — as you once thought it — has gone too far and you have been unjust to her, for which I am sorry to say, you will have to suffer hereafter along with others. Just now, on deck, your thoughts about her were dark and sinful, and so I find the moment a fitting one to put you on your guard.

Try to remove such misconceptions *as you will find*, by kind persuasion and an appeal to the feelings of loyalty to the Cause of truth if not to us. Make *all* these men feel that we have no favourites, nor affections for persons, but only for their good acts and humanity as a whole. But we employ agents — the best available. Of these for the past thirty years the chief has been the personality known as H. P. B. to the world (but otherwise to us). Imperfect and very troublesome, no doubt, she proves to some, nevertheless, there is no likelihood of our finding a better one for years to come — and your theosophists should be made to understand it. Since 1885 I have not written, nor caused to be written save thro' her agency, direct or remote, a letter or line to anybody in Europe or America, nor communicated orally *with*, or *thro'* any third party. Theosophists should learn it. You will understand later the significance of this declaration so keep it in mind. Her fidelity to our work being constant, and her sufferings having come upon her thro' it, neither I nor either of my Brother associates will desert or supplant her. As I once before remarked, *ingratitude* is not among our vices.

With yourself our relations are direct, and have been with the rare exceptions you know of, like the present, on the psychical plane, and so will continue thro' force of circumstances. That they are so rare — is your own fault as I told you in my last.

To help you in your present perplexity: H. P. B. has next to no concern with administrative details, and should be kept clear of them, so far as her strong nature can be controlled. But this *you must tell to all:* — *With occult matters she has everything to do.* We have *not*

---

[21] *Upāsika*, meaning "disciple," was a name often used by the Masters for H. P. Blavatsky.

abandoned her; she is *not* "given over to chelas." She is *our direct agent.* I warn you against permitting your suspicions and resentment against "her many follies" to bias your intuitive loyalty to her. In the adjustment of this European business, you will have two things to consider — the external and administrative, and the internal and psychical. Keep the former under your control and that of your most prudent associates, jointly; *leave the latter to her.* You are left to devise the practical details with your usual ingenuity. Only be careful, I say, to discriminate when some emergent interference of hers in practical affairs is referred to you on appeal, between that which is merely exoteric in origin and effects, and that which beginning on the practical tends to beget consequences on the spiritual plane. As to the former you are the best judge, as to the latter, she.

I have also noted, your thoughts about the "Secret Doctrine." Be assured that what she has not *annotated* from scientific and other works, we have given or *suggested* to her. Every mistake or erroneous notion, corrected and explained by her from the works of other theosophists *was corrected by me, or under my instruction.* It is a more valuable work than its predecessor, an epitome of occult truths that will make it a source of information and instruction for the earnest student for long years to come. . . .

You had better not mention for the present this letter to anyone — not even to H.P.B. unless she speaks to you of it herself. Time enough when you see occasion arise. It is merely given you, as a warning and a guide; to others, as a warning only, for you may use it discreetly if needs be.[22] — K.H.

Olcott arrived in London in late August 1888, to find H. P. Blavatsky not well and with much to do. A few weeks later on October 3rd he wrote Judge that he was busy helping her with *The Secret Doctrine* and *Lucifer* and in settling affairs in Paris — that he was acting "on the lines" of the letter he received from K.H. on board the *Shannon.*

The formation of the Esoteric Section was announced by H. S. Olcott, President in Council, attested to by H. P. Blavatsky, in the October and November issues of *Lucifer*, its introductory paragraph including the significant phrase "to be organized on the ORIGINAL LINES devised by the *real* founders of the T. S." — an indication of H.P.B.'s

---

[22] *Letters from the Masters of the Wisdom,* First Series, Letter 19, 5th edition.

continuing effort to bring the Society again under the influence of the Adepts.²³ At the Convention held December 1888 at Adyar, Olcott remarked that he as President would now reassume all responsibility he had for several years held jointly with the Executive Council for the "practical management for keeping the Society moving forward in its chosen line of usefulness." It was his business, he said, to "keep alive the body which contains the indwelling spirit called Theosophy," for he had never set himself up as "a competent teacher. That is Madame Blavatsky's speciality." Therefore he had "issued an Order . . . creating an Esoteric Section under her sole direction, as a body, or group, entirely separate and distinct from the Society proper, . . ."²⁴ The establishment of the Esoteric Section, however, in time brought to the fore Olcott's difficulty in comprehending H.P.B.'s relation to the theosophical endeavor, and this inability to recognize her real position roused his doubts regarding her motives. He was fearful that the esoteric work would divide the Society and take away its power.

Members in America, however, were seeking to join the Esoteric Section in such numbers that Judge, concerned that they did not understand its altruistic purposes, took his question to Mme. Blavatsky. Dr. A. Keightley gave her reply in his letter of September 11, 1889:

> She said that you were perfectly right and yet as wrong. The work being done is for the future the next century as I understood her. She is as well aware as you that promiscuous gathering of E S is no good but she says that it is absolutely necessary to have a large mass from which the people will themselves select themselves and thus both T.S. and E.S. will have to be wide open to give every one the chance of proving what he or she is made of. . . .

He closes his letter with the following comment:

> H.P.B. says that Master is going to answer your letter to her.

---

²³ Inevitably, "bogus Esoteric and Occult Societies" came forward at this time, which H. P. B. in her 1889 letter refers to as "our most insidious foes." Against this pseudo-theosophy she protested vigorously; see *Lucifer*, March 1889, pp. 1–12.

²⁴ *General Report of the Thirteenth Convention and Anniversary of the Theosophical Society*, Adyar, Madras, December 27-29, 1888, pp. 3-4.

With *The Secret Doctrine* published and the Esoteric Section functioning in Europe and the United States, Mme. Blavatsky poured her considerable energies into work in the West, which grew at a pace almost too fast to control, particularly in America. She also wrote *The Key to Theosophy* (1889), an introduction to the basic concepts which was most needed to correct misconceptions about the Society and the origin of its teachings. This was followed shortly by *The Voice of the Silence*, a devotional book for earnest students. She prepared study material for the esoteric students, conducted a large correspondence, edited and wrote regularly for *Lucifer*, and contributed articles to a number of other theosophical periodicals, while the Theosophical Publishing Society, largely run by Countess Wachtmeister assisted by Judge in America, greatly expanded its activities. There were also interviews with H. P. Blavatsky and meetings both public and private, at which she answered questions. In the early months of 1889 a series of studies on the Stanzas of Dzyan from the first volume of *The Secret Doctrine* were held, and these were later edited and published as *Transactions of the Blavatsky Lodge*.

This same year in August Olcott visited Europe again, in the hope of meeting the increasing demand by the Western Sections for more autonomy in conducting their work. For several months there had been much discussion in *The Theosophist* and *Lucifer*, and also in correspondence as to whether there should be a dominant central Headquarters which would legislate all matters and to which all members would turn as the "center" of the work, or whether there should be greater independence of action for the various sectors of the Society. The report of the British Section General Council of 18th December 1889 states that the following recommendation was proposed, and that President Olcott, who was present at the meeting, signified his willingness to give "the required authority to Madame Blavatsky and the Council he should appoint to assist her."

> In consequence of the great distance of the British Section from Headquarters, it is considered advisable that H. P. Blavatsky, assisted by a Council appointed by Col. Olcott, should be authorized to deal on emergency with any questions that may arise which are properly referable to the President, as the delay caused by the length of time that

must elapse before answer can be obtained from India might give rise to serious and even disastrous consequences to the Section. . . .[25]

As the months went by, however, the relation of the President-Founder to the Lodges and members in Britain and on the continent remained remote. Therefore, at the request of "the active Lodges in Europe, and . . . a large majority of the Unattached Fellows," Mme. Blavatsky reluctantly abandoned her position of remaining apart from the administration of T. S. affairs, and assumed the direct responsibility for the European work. In the July *Lucifer* for 1890 appeared the following announcement:

NOTICE.

IN OBEDIENCE TO THE ALMOST UNANIMOUS VOICE OF THE FELLOWS OF THE THEOSOPHICAL SOCIETY IN EUROPE, I, H. P. BLAVATSKY, THE ORIGINATOR AND CO-FOUNDER OF THE THEOSOPHICAL SOCIETY, ACCEPT THE DUTY OF EXERCISING THE PRESIDENTIAL AUTHORITY FOR THE WHOLE OF EUROPE; AND IN VIRTUE OF THIS AUTHORITY I DECLARE THAT THE HEADQUARTERS OF THE THEOSOPHICAL SOCIETY IN LONDON, WHERE I RESIDE, WILL IN FUTURE BE THE HEADQUARTERS FOR THE TRANSACTION OF ALL OFFICIAL BUSINESS OF THE THEOSOPHICAL SOCIETY IN EUROPE.

H. P. BLAVATSKY

Let no one imagine that this reform in any sense suggests a separation from, or even to the loosening in any way of the authority of, my colleague at Adyar. Colonel H. S. Olcott remains, as heretofore, the President-Founder of the Theosophical Society *the world over*. But it has been found impossible for him at such a great distance to exercise accurate discrimination in current matters of guidance of the Theosophical Society. . . .

Olcott felt that the European Section had been "irregularly formed," as he later wrote Judge. Therefore, to legalize the matter, he issued an official order on July 9, 1890, requesting that a European Section be established giving H. P. Blavatsky "full management" of the same.

---

[25] *Supplement to The Theosophist*, March 1890, p. cvii.

The new Section received the same autonomy as the American Section.[26]

Meanwhile in America at the Section headquarters Judge and his few helpers worked long hours with T. S. and E. S. correspondence, issuing books, pamphlets, and tracts, as well as getting out his monthly journal, *The Path*. In 1889 a printing press was purchased by New York and Chicago theosophists and supported by the American members. With this assistance the publishing program was substantially augmented. Several small magazines were distributed for the aid of Branches and members at large: *The Theosophical Forum*, in which Judge and various students answered questions; *Department of Branch Work*, which circularized Papers read at Branch meetings throughout the country; and later, the series of *Oriental Department* Papers which featured translations from Sanskrit literature. *Yoga Aphorisms* by Patañjali with an introduction by W. Q. Judge also appeared, followed in 1890 by *Echoes From the Orient*, the *Bhagavad Gita*, and *Letters That Have Helped Me* (volume 1). Because of the success of their publishing activities, a larger printing press was purchased and sent to London with a New York member, James M. Pryse, to man it.

There were many dedicated theosophists supporting H.P.B. in her last years, but none were more responsive to the inner lines of her endeavor than William Q. Judge. He seemed to anticipate the needs of the work she so desperately wished to accomplish and, in different ways, to provide her with the means to carry it out. We should not be surprised at his insight and dedication in light of her letters to him during these years, from which we make the following selection. On October 3, 1886 she had written him:

> The trouble with you is *that you do not know the great change* that came to pass in you a few years ago. Others have occasionally their *astrals* changed & replaced by those of Adepts (as of Elementaries) & they influence the *outer*, and the *higher* man. With you it is the *Nirmanakaya* not the "astral" that blended with your astral. Hence the dual nature & fighting.

The next year Judge received a cable from H.P.B., dated London,

---

[26] *Supplement to The Theosophist*, August 1890, p. 9.

August 12, 1887, reading as follows: "MASTER SUGGESTS YOUR BEING WHAT I AM SECRETARY FOR LIFE IF READY FOR SACRIFICE HE WILL HELP. [*signed*] UPASIKA." Judge has written on the cable: "Reply — Ready. What is nature of sacrifice Secretary here or where when."

On October 23, 1889, about a year after the formation of the Esoteric Section, H.P.B. wrote to Judge:

> The Esoteric Section and its life in the U.S.A. depends on W.Q.J. remaining its agent & what he is now. The day W.Q.J. resigns, H.P.B. will be virtually dead for the Americans. W.Q.J. is the *Antaskarana* [bridge] between the two Manas(es) the American thought & the Indian — or rather the trans-Himalayan Esoteric Knowledge. DIXI
>
> H.P.B. ∴
>
> P.S. W.Q.J. had better show, & impress *this* on the mind *of all those whom it may concern* H.P.B.

In these last years of H. P. Blavatsky's life had come the flood of teaching so important to the world. Theosophy was neither Oriental nor Occidental, but rather a restatement of the eternal tradition, the fountainhead of wisdom. These concepts were not new to the Eastern mind, but there was the hope of awakening sleeping Asia to individual religious freedom for all her peoples, regardless of caste or sex. It was a new revelation to the West, however, a land of materialism in science and theology which offered little fulfillment for those searching for spiritual values, and no valid explanation of psychism.

The span of time lends perspective, and we can now, more than a century later, envision to some extent H. P. Blavatsky's relation to the Theosophical Society and her struggle to keep it from becoming but another organization outside the influence of her teachers. We can also understand why she wrote as she did to the American members and gave honor to William Q. Judge as one able to appreciate her true position, and the deeper import of the theosophical purpose: the establishment of a vehicle through which would pour the spiritual vitality and ideas necessary to uplift the human race, not only in her time and the century coming, but through the whole of the Messianic cycle ahead. To this she gave her life.

Index

Asterisk (*) indicates reference material is in footnote.

Adepts, 5, 18, 58, 61, 65, 68. *See also* Master(s)
Adyar, 8, 27, 51*, 53, 56, 59-60
Allahabad, 52
Altruism, 16, 18-19, 29
America (United States), 3, 8-9, 16, 27, 43, 56, 63, 65
American Board of Control, 59
American Section, 6, 16, 47-50, 59-60, 68-9
Anglo-Indian community, 51
Animalism, 6
Animals, cruelty to, 7
Antaskarana, 69
Arya-Samaj of Arya-wart, 50

Bellamy, Edward, 29*
"Benjamin," 56
Besant, Annie, 26, 35, 38, 43
Bhagavad Gita, 68
Black Magic, 18, 29
Blavatsky, H. P.
  agent of Adepts, 63-4
  books by, 66
  Corresponding Secretary, 48*, 55
  Coulomb affair and, 53-5
  differences between Olcott and, 54-6, 58-9, 62-4
  Esoteric Section and, 61-2, 64-5
  in America, 47-8
  in Europe, 56-8, 66-7
  in India, 50-1
  Judge and, 68-9
  "Miracle Club" and, 4*
  reestablish work, 58-9
  T.S. during years of retirement, 49-50

Blavatsky, H. P. (cont.)
  U.S. citizen, 9, 33
  views on leaving India 1885, 55-6
Blavatsky Lodge, 26, 66
Board of Control (Adyar), 53
Bombay, 51*
Boston scandals, 21
Bouton, J. W., 50*
Branches, 6, 15, 20, 25-6, 33, 51. *See also* Isis Branch, Pacific Coast Branches
British Section, 20, 35, 60-1, 66-7
Brotherhood, 5, 7, 17, 20-1, 34, 48. *See also* Universal Brotherhood
  Great Ideal, 7
Buck, Dr., 21
Buddhism, 15, 51, 53
Burrows, Herbert, 26

Center, each person as a, 4
Ceylon (Sri Lanka), 51, 53
Charity, 6-8
Charlatans, 21
Chelas, 64
  selection of, 61
"Chelas and Lay Chelas" (H. P. Blavatsky), 61-2
Christian College Magazine, The, 52-3
Christianity, 15, 20
Christian Science, 28-9
Clairvoyance, 18
Collins, Mabel (Mabel Cook), 7, 57
Cook, Mabel. *See* Collins, Mabel
Corson, Prof. Hiram, 48
Coues, Dr. Elliott, 17-18, 49
Coulomb, M. and Mme., 53, 55-6
Curtis, 49

Cycle
  ending 1897-8, 33
  Messianic, 69
  new, 3, 25, 28-9

D'Adhémar, Countess, 21
Daly, Bowles, 27
Dead, worship of, 5, 17
Department of Branch Work, 68
Disunion, 34
Djual Kul, 56
Doubleday, General Abner, 49-50
Drunkenness, 7
Dzyan, Stanzas of, 66

Echoes from the Orient (W. Q. Judge), 68
Elberfeld, Germany, 55
Enemies, 17-19, 21, 34
England, 7-9, 16, 26, 33, 35, 53
  H.P.B. moves to, 57
Esoteric Buddhism (A. P. Sinnett), 52
Esoteric School, 61
Esoteric Section, 21, 27, 29, 61-2, 69
  founding of, 64-6
Ethics, Morality, 16-17, 29, 48
Europe, 34, 53, 55-6, 63, 66
European Section, 35, 60, 67-8

Fawcett, E. D., 27
Fludd, 61
Founders of T.S., 7-8, 27
  real, 18, 64

Genii of Nations, Knowledge(s), and Religion(s) (G.N.K.R.), 19

Hartmann, Dr. Franz, 55
Headquarters, issue of central, 66-7
Healing, 28-9
Hermetic Brotherhood of Luxor (H.B. of L.), 19
Hodgson, Richard, 54-5
Humanity, helping, 4, 7, 22, 27, 29
Hume, A. O., 52
Hypnotism, 18
Hypocrisy, 6

India, 9, 15, 27, 34, 48, 50-1, 53, 55
Ireland, 27
Isis Branch (Paris), 62
Isis Unveiled (H. P. Blavatsky), 8, 48, 56

Japan, 15-16
Jesus, 21
Judge, William Quan, 3, 7, 24-5, 43, 47-50, 56, 62, 65-9
  at Adyar, 53
  differences with H. S. Olcott, 59-60

Karma, 20, 22, 29
Keightley, Archibald, 57, 60, 65
Keightley, Bertram, 25, 57-8
Key to Theosophy, The (H. P. Blavatsky), 66
K.H., 52
  views on *The Secret Doctrine*, 64
  views on T.S., 62-4
Kingsford, Dr. Anna, 53

Letters That Have Helped Me (W. Q. Judge), 68
Library (Adyar), 60
Literature, distribution of, 7
Lodges, 6-7, 20. *See also* Blavatsky Lodge, London Lodge
London, 26, 68
London Lodge, 53, 56, 62
Looking Backward, 2000–1887 (E. Bellamy), 29*
Lotus, Le, 21
Lucifer, 7, 20, 26, 35, 38, 58, 64, 66-7

M., 52
Magic, 18. *See also* Black Magic
Mahatmas. *See* Master(s)
Mānasic development and psychism, 35
Mankind. *See* Humanity
Master(s), Mahatmas, 19, 27-8, 52-3, 56, 61-2, 65, 69
  quoted, 22, 62-4
Materialism, 5-6, 17, 21, 38, 48
Maynard, 49
Mead, G. R. S., 19*
Mediums, 18

INDEX 73

Meeting Hall, new, 26
Mesmerism, 18
Metaphysical Healing, 28-9
Mind Cure, 28-9
Miracle Club, 4
Missionaries, 51-3

Nationalist Movement, 29
New York, 15, 47, 59
  Branch, 49
Nirmāṇakāya, 68

Objectives of T.S., 47-8, 51-2
Occultism, Occultists, 5-6, 18
Occult World, The (A. P. Sinnett), 52
Olcott, Henry S., 4*, 9, 15-16, 20-1, 26-7, 65-7
  administration of T.S. and, 64
  Coulomb affair and, 53-4
  differences between Blavatsky and, 58-9, 62-4
  differences between Judge and, 60
  in America, 47-8
  in Asia, 50-1
  meets Sinnett, 52
  relation of, to Adepts, 63
Oriental Department Papers, 68
Orthodoxy, 5
Ostend, Belgium, 57

Pacific Coast Branches, 26
Paracelsus, 61
Paris, 47, 62, 64
Patañjali, 68
Path, The, 6, 20, 60, 68
Paul, 20
Pehio [Pei Ho], S.S., letter, 55
Personality, 21
Phenomena
  psychic, 4, 16, 52-3
  psychological, 18
Phenomenalism, 4-5
Pico della Mirandola, 61
Pioneer, The, 52
Politics, 7
Powell, 27
Powers, psychic and occult, 28

Prāna, 28
Prejudice, 7, 17, 21
Pride, 34
Printing Press, 68
Pryse, James M., 68
Psychic
  cravings, 5
  phenomena, 16, 52-3
  powers, 28
  studies, 18
Psychism, in America, 16, 35

Reincarnation, 29
Revue Théosophique, La, 21
Root-race, 35
Rosicrucians, 18
Row, Subba, 56

St. Germain, Count, 61
Sanskrit, 51
Saraswati, Swami Dya Nand (Dayanand), 50
Science, 48
Secret Doctrine, The (H. P. Blavatsky), 8, 53, 56-8, 64, 66
Sects, 5, 19
Selfishness, 6, 29
Separateness, 19
Shannon, S.S., letter, 62-4
Simla, 52
Sinnett, A. P., 52-3
Society for Psychical Research, 7, 54
Solidarity, 17, 21, 27
Soup Kitchens, 8
Spirit, materialization of, 6
Spiritists, 17
Spiritual
  development and psychism, 35
  healing, 28-9
Spiritualism, Spiritualists, 4, 17, 47
Sticks, bundle of, 34
Sub-race, 28, 35

Theology, 48
Theosophical Forum, The, 68
Theosophical Publication Society (T.P.S.), 7, 20, 66

Theosophical Society
  Adepts and, 6, 27, 47, 52, 55, 58, 60-1, 62-4, 65
  Adepts' views on, 58
  Adyar and Western Sections of, 59-60
  founded, 15, 47
  function of, 6-8
  growth of Sections of, 6, 15-16, 20-2, 25, 26, 33, 49-50, 51, 56, 59-60, 64-8
  in West, 3, 9, 27, 56, 59-60, 66
  reoriented, 18
  Section autonomy in, 6, 59-60, 66-7
  state of, 18-20, 21, 58, 60, 62-4, 65-7
Theosophist, The, 50, 56, 66
Theosophy, 3-5, 7
  practical realization of, 29
Tract Mailing Scheme, 26
Transactions of the Blavatsky Lodge, 66

Unanimity, 28
Union, Unity, 20-1, 25, 28, 34-5

United Kingdom. *See* British Section, England
United States. *See* America
Universal Brotherhood, 18-19, 21, 26-7, 29, 51. *See also* Brotherhood
Upāsika, 63, 69

Vanity, 34
Vaughan, Thomas, 61
Voice of the Silence, The, 66

Wachtmeister, Countess, 7, 57, 66
Weisse, 49
Western Society for Psychic Research, 18
Wilder, Dr. Alexander, 48-9
Wisdom-Religion, 18
Women, injustice to, 7
Würzburg, Germany, 57

Yoga Aphorisms (Patañjali), 68